Egypt and Nubia

JOHN H. TAYLOR

HARVARD UNIVERSITY PRESS

Cambridge, Massachusetts

1991

Copyright © 1991
by The Trustees of the
British Museum

ISBN 0-674-24130-4

Library of Congress Catalog
Card Number 91-71308

Printed in Hong Kong

Front cover Sphinx of Taharqo (690–664 BC) from Temple 'T' at Kawa. L. 74.7 cm.

Back cover Ring-flask decorated with guilloche and floral motifs, from a Meroitic grave at Faras, first to second century AD. H. 23.2 cm.

Inside front cover Ruins of the Meroitic temple at Musawwarat es-Sufra.

Inside back cover Falcon-headed sphinx at the temple of Ramesses II, Wadi es-Sebua.

Title page Wall-painting from the tomb-chapel of Sebekhotep at Thebes. c.1400 BC, showing Nubians bringing gold rings, ebony logs, incense and other African luxury goods, to the Egyptian king.

This page Pyramids of Meroitic rulers in the northern cemetery at Meroe, third century BC to fourth century AD.

Contents

1 The Land of Nubia and Its Inhabitants

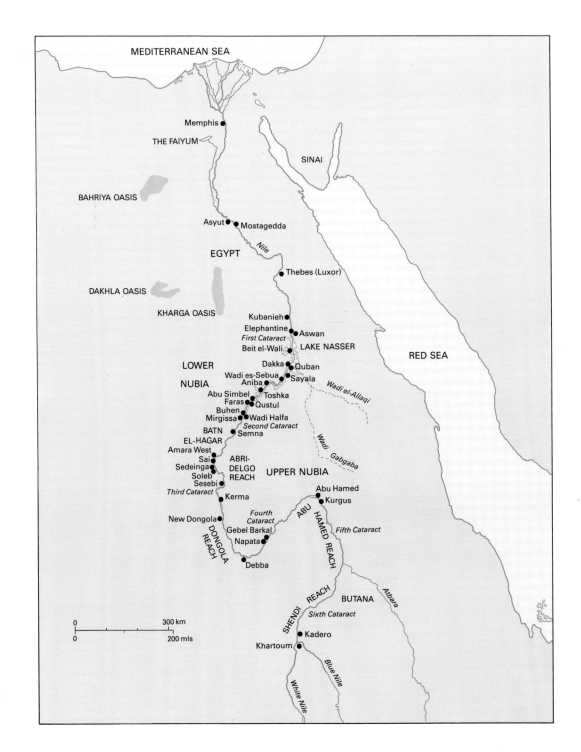

1 Egypt and Nubia, Neolithic period to New Kingdom, showing the principal sites.

2 Nubian landscape in the Batn el-Hagar.

The ancient land of Nubia, which is today divided between Egypt and the Republic of the Sudan, consisted in essence of the stretch of the Nile valley immediately south of Egypt. This was the only continuously occupied tract of land linking sub-Saharan Africa with the Mediterranean world, a position which was a crucial factor in shaping the course of Nubia's history.

In earlier times many different states and kingdoms flourished there and the region has been known by several names. Ironically, the name given to it by the earlier indigenous inhabitants is unknown. The Egyptians at different times called it *Ta-sety* ('Land of the Bow', a reference to the weapon most closely associated with the Nubians), 'the Southern Lands', or 'Kush'. To the Greeks and Romans, it was part of Ethiopia ('Land of Burnt Faces'), a vaguely defined region stretching from India to West Africa. The name 'Nubia', which first occurs in the Roman period, poses problems of interpretation, for while it is tempting to see it as a derivative of *nbw*, the Ancient Egyptian word for gold, its etymology has not been established conclusively. Although no political entity exists under this name today, the term 'Nubia' is still used to define the region between Aswan and Debba in which the Nubian languages are spoken. In ancient times, the peoples who spoke these languages and who were ethnically and culturally re-lated, inhabited the entire area from Aswan to Khartoum and beyond. It is in this wider sense that the term 'Nubia' is used in this book.

The Nile is the single most important feature of the Nubian landscape and, as in Egypt, its life-giving water was vital to the development of human settlement. On its northward journey from Khartoum the river passes through a constantly changing environment. For most of its course it flows over a soft sandstone bed which is periodically interrupted by rocky barriers of granite, forming the cataracts, where the channel is broken into dangerous and unnavigable rapids. Between the six main cataracts which lie between Khartoum and Aswan are contrasting landscapes. Areas with relatively rich alluvial deposits, such as the Dongola Reach and Lower Nubia, and the grasslands of the Shendi Reach, favoured human settlement and, predictably, it was here that the greatest cultural advances took place. The cataracts and the barren rocky stretches of the Batn el-Hagar ('Belly of Rocks') and the Abu Hamed Reach were only sporadically inhabited. As barriers to navigation they tended to become frontier zones, and important land routes developed to avoid them. The Batn el-Hagar marks the principal division into Upper and Lower Nubia, the southern and northern regions of the land respectively.

Today Nubia has one of the world's most extreme environments. Daytime temperatures can reach 52°C, rainfall is almost unknown north of Dongola, and harsh erosive winds blow all year round from the Sahara Desert. In antiquity it was not quite so forbidding: the climate was moister and in Upper Nubia savannah-like vegetation – which has now retreated further south due to increasing dessication – flourished as long ago as the fifth millennium BC. Against this backdrop emerged some of the earliest urbanised and culturally advanced societies in north-east Africa.

3 Section of a wall-painting from the tomb chapel of the Treasurer Sebekhotep at Thebes, *c.*1400 BC, showing Nubians presenting gold nuggets and rings to King Thutmose IV. H. 80 cm.

The historical importance of Nubia was primarily economic and stemmed, on the one hand, from the rich natural resources – chiefly gold, copper and stone but also semi-precious stones such as cornelian, jasper and amethyst – which were obtainable within easy reach of the Nile and more significantly, from the strategic location of the land itself as virtually the only reliable link between the lands of tropical Africa and the Mediterranean. It was along this 'corridor' that the wealth of Africa passed in trade: ivory, ebony, incense, exotic animals, slaves, and a host of other luxuries.

Because of these factors the Nubians were in close contact with their neighbours for long periods of their history, often profiting from their position as commercial middlemen, at other times being subjected to the domination of stronger powers. This was the pattern of their relationship with the Egyptians who, through their efforts to exploit and dominate the southern land, left a lasting impression on Nubian cultural development. In the long term, the relationship was reciprocal. Nubian culture influenced that of Egypt at several important periods and culminated in the domination of the northern kingdom by Nubian rulers at the end of the eighth century BC.

Egypt was not the only influence, however. Nubia's position made it a meeting-place of different cultures, and her own cultural make-up reflects a constantly changing mixture of indigenous and outside elements – on the one hand are the southern traditions which reflect the Nubians' links with the people of central Africa, and on the other the influence of the Mediterranean cultures with which they came into contact from time to time.

The modern Nubians are probably the direct descendants of the ancient inhabitants, since the physical characteristics of the people appear to have changed little over the millennia. The varying environmental conditions along the enormously long inhabited strip of the Nile valley are accurately reflected in the gradual if superficial change in the physical characteristics of the population from north to south, skin becoming darker in colour, facial features flatter, hair more tightly curled and skeletons increasingly slender. The ancient Egyptians observed these differences and faithfully reproduced them in painting and sculpture, distinguishing the 'brown'-skinned inhabitants of Lower Nubia from the black people living further to the south. The ancient Egyptians and the Nubians were closely linked in ethnic background, but the languages they spoke were unrelated. Whereas Ancient Egyptian was an Afro-Asiatic language (a family found in North and East Africa and in Western Asia), the Nubian tongues belonged to the Nilo-Saharan group, found only in the central part of the continent.

Archaeological excavation has made the largest contribution to our understanding of the history of Nubia. Three major archaeological surveys and many independent campaigns have been conducted, mainly in Lower Nubia, since the beginning of this century. The most ambitious enterprise, however, was the Unesco rescue campaign of 1960–80, organised in response to the construction of the Aswan High Dam, which resulted in the permanent flooding of Lower Nubia. Involving the systematic excavation of scores of archaeological sites and the physical removal and re-erection of the temples destined to be submerged beneath the waters of Lake Nasser, it emphasised the necessity of salvaging cultural heritage, and has made the archaeology of Lower Nubia probably the best documented of any comparable area in the world.

Written evidence is rare. No Nubian language was written down until the second century BC, when the Meroitic script was devised (see below). Since even this remains largely untranslatable, the ancient Nubians cannot speak for themselves, and the scholar is forced to view them through the writings of the various foreigners with whom they came into contact. The majority of the textual sources, therefore, incorporate a degree of bias and, even when not actually hostile to the Nubians, are often confused or exaggerated.

The first synthesis of Nubian cultural development was devised in the early years of this century by the American archaeologist George Andrew Reisner, of the Harvard University–Museum of Fine Arts, Boston Expedition, who distinguished the different phases by names such as 'A-Group', 'B-Group' and 'C-Group'. The basis of this division was the changes observable in material culture, but Reisner's use of the term 'group' reflected an erroneous belief that the alterations in customs and types of artifact were accompanied by physical changes in the population. The emergence of each new phase was seen as the result of an incursion or migration of 'new' people, whose culture ousted that of their precursors. In place of Reisner's 'Groups' some recent scholars prefer to substitute 'phases', 'sequences' or 'horizons'. The emphasis on cultural continuity which this approach entails undoubtedly clarifies the picture of Nubian history, but the terms 'A-Group' and 'C-Group' have now become so well established in the archaeological literature as a means of distinguishing assemblages of material remains that they have been retained in this book.

2 Early Nubian Cultures and the Egyptian Old Kingdom

In the late Palaeolithic period, from c.25,000 BC, both Egypt and Nubia were inhabited by nomadic bands who lived in small temporary camps close to the Nile and depended for their survival on hunting wild animals and fishing in the abundantly stocked river. The principal material remains of these earliest inhabitants are their stone tools and numerous drawings on the rocks along the valley, showing the animals they hunted: giraffe, antelope, elephant and gazelle.

By the Mesolithic and Neolithic periods there was a trend towards the establishment of settled societies, and numerous localised cultures arose in different parts of Egypt and Nubia. A notable development which occurred at this time was the beginning of pottery production, itself an indication of an increasingly sedentary society. Knowledge of ceramics first became established in the Khartoum and Shendi regions of the Nile valley towards 6000 BC with a culture known as the Khartoum Mesolithic. The handmade ceramics of these people are unpainted globular vessels decorated with wavy line and dotted

4 Fragments of the earliest Nubian ceramics: 'wavy line' pottery of the Khartoum Mesolithic culture (top) and 'dotted wavy line' sherds of the Neolithic (bottom). H. of upper fragment 6.7 cm.

zigzag motifs, impressed into the clay with a fishbone or rocker-stamp. These techniques became more sophisticated in the succeeding Khartoum Neolithic phase, and the surface of the pottery was usually burnished.

Whereas their precursors had subsisted by hunting and fishing, the Khartoum Neolithic people were the first in this region to keep domesticated cattle and to cultivate cereal crops. These methods of subsistence were apparently introduced into the Nile valley from the eastern Sahara and were being practised at the important site of Kadero, north of Khartoum, as early as c.4000 BC. Although other cultures with a related ceramic tradition continued to flourish in adjacent areas like the eastern Sudan, the Khartoum Neolithic culture itself came to an end in the early third millennium BC and the central Nile valley was apparently left unoccupied for over two thousand years. It is in Lower Nubia that the next important cultural developments can be most clearly traced.

Food production and the domestication of animals may have been practised in Lower Nubia as early as the fourth millennium BC, though the evidence is not conclusive. The early cultures there seem to have had more in common with those of Upper Egypt than with the Khartoum region, and it was perhaps from Egypt that they learned about the new subsistence methods. Some of the early Lower Nubian cultures had a definite influence on the development of important stages of early Upper Egyptian culture at this time. Comparison between the pottery of the Abkan Culture of the Second Cataract area and that of the Badarian, the dominant culture of Upper Egypt between c.5000 and c.4500 BC, indicates that both were closely related, an impression reinforced by the similarity of their methods of making tools and the sources they used for raw materials. Conversely the Nagada Culture of Upper Egypt was influential in

northern Nubia, as seen in the presence of Nagada objects in Lower Nubian graves and similarities in pottery design.

The first widespread indigenous Nubian culture, the A-Group, developed between *c.*3500 and *c.*3000 BC. It extended throughout Lower Nubia from Kubanieh, north of Aswan, to the Second Cataract region and it owed a great deal both to the earlier cultures which had existed in the same area, notably the Abkan Culture, and to those of predynastic Egypt.

The A-Group Nubians, like their predecessors, lived a semi-nomadic life. Communities probably consisted of a few families dwelling in temporary camps of reed or grass huts, and moving with the seasons. It is likely that they lived close to the banks of the Nile for most of the year, moving back to the edge of the floodplain when the river overflowed its banks during the annual inundation. Rock-shelters were also used, and towards the end of the fourth millennium permanent settlements, sometimes with stone houses, were becoming increasingly common.

During the A-Group period agriculture became more widespread. Cereals and leguminous plants were grown on the floodplain and grinding stones of sandstone or quartzite were used to prepare the grain. Animal husbandry may also have been practised, though the scarcity of firm evidence makes it hard to assess its importance. Sheep and goats and a few cattle were probably the main animals kept, but hunting, gathering and fishing were still an important means of obtaining food.

The close contacts which existed between the inhabitants of southern Egypt and northern Nubia at this period must have been based largely on trade. Before the end of the fourth millennium BC Egyptian craftsmen were already working ivory and ebony to produce figurines, amulets, ornamental containers and furniture fittings, and much of the raw

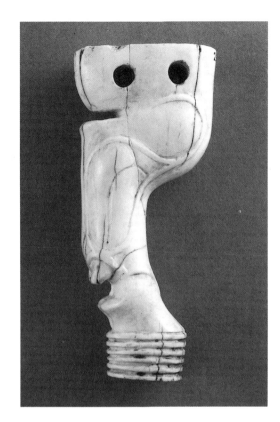

5 Furniture fitment in the form of a bull's leg, probably made from elephant ivory. Pieces such as this formed parts of beds and chairs and have been found in several Egyptian graves of the First and Second Dynasties. H. 11.4 cm.

materials presumably came from the south. The main Egyptian market for this trade was probably on the island of Elephantine at Aswan. The very name of the place (in Egyptian, *Abu*, 'Elephant Town', translated into 'Elephantine' by the Greeks) indicates that it was a major emporium for traffic in ivory and doubtless for other African products. The A-Group Nubians probably acted as middlemen in this trade, and the contents of their graves provide information on the kinds of goods which the Egyptians supplied in return. Egyptian beer- and wine-jars are frequently found, suggesting that these drinks – probably not made in Nubia – were much sought after. Food products, such as cheese, oil and honey, as well as linen cloth were doubtless also traded. Copper axes and adzes of Egyptian type are

6 (*Above*) Copper axe head imported from Egypt and found in an A-Group grave at Faras. It was wrapped in woven matting or basketry, traces of which are visible adhering to the surface. L. 12.3 cm.

7 (*Above right*) Grave of an A-Group Nubian excavated in the cemetery at Faras. The gifts for the deceased include a cosmetic palette, placed in front of the face, vessels to contain food and drink, and stone grinders for crushing grain.

found in the richer graves, and smaller metal implements such as awls and needles may also have come from Egypt. Some graves are remarkable for the richness of their contents. The best-known example is the grave at Sayala in which were found two gold-handled ceremonial maces, copper chisels and fine stone vessels and palettes of Egyptian type. It is conjectured that this grave may have been that of a chief who had received presents from Egyptian trading partners. While the degree of variation in A-Group graves and their contents is insufficient to suggest the existence of a truly stratified society, the Sayala burial was not the only one which contained rich goods. A cemetery of this period at Qustul, near Faras, which yielded exceptionally rich goods, may be the burial place of other chiefs who profited by trade with Egypt.

The A-Group graves were usually oval or 7 rectangular pits with circular stone super-

structures. They are the first in Lower Nubia in which objects were buried with the dead, and 8 in the absence of written records their contents tell us most of what is known about the beliefs and lifestyle of the people. Items of personal adornment are commonly found; necklaces, 9 amulets and pendants were made from shell, ivory, bone, faience and stone. Bracelets and anklets were usually of bone or stone, though sometimes of ostrich-eggshell or ivory. As in Egypt, green eye-paint made from malachite was used by both sexes; many graves have yielded the rhomboidal quartzite palettes and 10 the pebbles which were used to grind the pigment. A few graves contained simple garments such as belts and leather loincloths. Feathers were worn in the hair and sometimes leather caps are found.

The most attractive class of objects found at A-Group sites is the pottery. Ceramics were generally more highly valued by the Nubians than the Egyptians throughout the period covered by this book, a circumstance which is reflected in the technical and artistic superiority of Nubian pottery. The handmade ceramics of the A-Group include pots with a polished red exterior and a shiny black interior and rim, the surfaces often decorated with a rippled finish. The finest type, however, is the 'eggshell' pottery. Examples are mostly 11 open bowls and cups, with very thin walls (3–5 mm), decorated on the outside with geometric patterns or designs derived from basketry, painted in red ochre. Vessels of this type are relatively rare and must have been highly prized.

A-Group craftsmen also produced clay figurines of humans and animals, which represent a considerable advance in artistic expression and are among the earliest examples of sculpture in the round from Nubia. The human figurines, probably intended to fulfil some magical role, are steatopygous females with attenuated limbs and very summary

8 (*Left*) Selection of objects from the grave shown in fig.7, including grinding stones and a large redware bowl. The tall jar and the pot with painted decoration at the neck are Egyptian imports. H. of tall jar 45 cm.

9 (*Above, top*) String of white shell beads, perhaps intended as an anklet, from an A-Group grave at Faras. L. 23.5 cm.

10 (*Above*) White quartzite cosmetic palette with traces of the green pigment which was ground on its surface and used as eye paint. The use of quartzite and the rhomboidal shape typify the palettes of the A-Group. From Faras. L. 9.5 cm.

11 A-Group 'eggshell' vessels from Faras. These thin-walled handmade pots are decorated with red ochre, the designs ranging from spots printed with a finger (right) to intricate patterns inspired by basketwork (left). H. 15.4 cm and 12.2 cm.

facial features. Linear markings on the abdominal area and on the thighs are thought to represent some form of body decoration such as tattooing.

Because of the harsh environment of Lower Nubia the population remained small and scattered; consequently development towards an urbanised and stratified society was slow. Egypt, in contrast, experienced a rapid rise to a high level of cultural development during the late fourth millennium BC. With the unification of the country under a single ruler in c.3100 BC, Egypt emerged as a hierarchical society with a centralised government, a written language and expanding commercial interests abroad. As territorial boundaries became more firmly defined, the First Cataract came to be regarded as a political frontier between Egypt and Nubia. With growing Egyptian prosperity and cultural sophistication, demand for southern luxury goods increased and rulers turned more and more to aggression in order to obtain what had formerly been acquired through trade. Raids into Nubia took place in the First Dynasty and seem to have increased in frequency and scale during the Old Kingdom (c.2686–2181 BC). The A-Group chiefs who had profited by acting as intermediaries in the trade now found themselves bypassed as the Egyptians sought to make contact directly with the markets further south.

The A-Group culture, which had reached its peak in the Egyptian First Dynasty (c. 3100–2890 BC), came to an end in the early third millennium, and the following centuries are almost a blank in the archaeological record of northern Nubia. Thinly scattered groups of indigenous people perhaps continued to occupy the region as late as the Fourth or Fifth Dynasty but the majority of inhabitants of Lower Nubia seem to have abandoned the Nile valley and retreated to the desert edges, forced to leave their homes by a deterioration in the climate and the effects of the change in Egyptian policy from a mutually beneficial exchange system to one of exploitation.

The Egyptians' new aggressive attitude also entailed the establishment of permanent settlements to exploit Nubia's natural resources more effectively. The earliest one yet identified is a walled town situated north of the Middle Kingdom fortress of Buhen, which flourished during the Fourth and Fifth Dynasties, though perhaps founded earlier. Copper was smelted there, as the remains of furnaces, crucibles, ingot moulds and quantities of slag and ore found on the site show. At the same period diorite and possibly cornelian was being extracted from quarries in the desert west of Toshka.

During the Egyptian Sixth Dynasty (c. 2345–2181 BC) Lower Nubia was resettled by a new culture, known as the C-Group (the existence of a 'B-Group', once thought to be the successor to the A-Group, has now been disproved). The C-Group culture remained dominant in the north until the people there were encouraged to adopt Egyptian customs in the sixteenth century BC. Though stemming from the same cultural tradition as the A-Group, the C-Group did not develop directly from the earlier phase; the precise origins of the people who reoccupied northern Nubia at this time are uncertain, but it is probable that they had moved in from the Western Desert.

The early C-Group people, while practising agriculture and hunting, were more strongly orientated towards cattle-herding than their predecessors. Though this has to be deduced from relatively isolated circumstances – the carving of long-horned cows on 'stelae' or grave markers, on pottery and on rocks, the burying of ox-skulls in cemeteries, and the use of cow-dung to temper pottery – there can be little doubt of the importance of cattle to these people. Sheep and goats were also kept.

While occupying much the same area as the A-Group, they enjoyed a more settled life. Important C-Group sites like Aniba, Faras and Dakka show long-term occupation over many generations. Huts and tents, seasonally occupied, were gradually replaced by houses consisting partly of drystone walls, with the upper parts of wattle and the roof supported by beams.

The burial practices of the C-Group were similar to those of the A-Group. The bodies were laid in round or oval pits in a semi-flexed position, and over these were built superstructures consisting of rings of stones filled with gravel. In some important cemeteries, such as that at Aniba, stone slabs were planted vertically in the ground to serve as stelae. The grave goods reveal both continuity and change in the customs of daily life. Clothing continued to consist chiefly of leather garments and sandals, while jewellery was confined mainly to necklaces and bangles, but the cosmetic palettes and pebbles, so characteristic of A-Group and early Egyptian graves, are absent.

The pottery of the C-Group is highly distinctive and, though handmade, shows high technical excellence. Some of it has clear affinities with Egyptian types, such as the black-topped red ware, also associated with the A-Group and the Kerma and Pan-Grave

12

12 (*Right*) Sandstone stelae erected over graves in the C-Group cemetery at Aniba. The largest are over 2 m high. Such stelae are known from several C-Group sites and are sometimes decorated with carvings of cattle.

13 (*Below*) C-Group bowl of polished incised ware from Faras. H. 8.1 cm.

Cultures (see below). The manufacture and decoration of other types, however, display African influence more strongly. An example is the 'polished incised ware'. These vessels are mainly round-bottomed bowls, probably used to hold food and drink, whose surfaces present a contrasting mosaic of smooth areas or stripes, and areas filled with hatched lines, criss-cross or herringbone patterns, the early examples probably deriving from basketwork designs. They were fired so as to leave a black or occasionally red lustrous surface, and white pigment was rubbed into the incisions to make the pattern stand out. C-Group graves also yield clay figurines of women and cattle.

About the time of the resettlement of Lower Nubia the character of Egyptian activity in the area changed. Operations at the Toshka quarries and the town at Buhen ceased in the late Fifth Dynasty (*c.*2400 BC) and the settle-

14 View across the Nile at Qubbet el-Hawa, Aswan. The cliffs on the west bank contain the rock-cut tombs of Harkhuf and other Egyptian governors who led expeditions into Nubia during the Sixth Dynasty.

ments seem to have been abandoned. No doubt the appearance of settlers obliged the Egyptians to adopt a different approach, as they now needed the co-operation of the C-Group to obtain Lower Nubian goods and to pass through on their way to trade with regions further south. It was to the provincial governors of Aswan that responsibility for maintaining this traffic now fell. These men acted as expedition-leaders, and the accounts of their exploits, inscribed in their tombs at Qubbet el-Hawa, provide an illuminating glimpse of conditions in Lower Nubia in this period. Three distinct regions are mentioned – Wawat, Irtjet and Satju – the chiefs of which probably traded cattle with the Egyptians, who also mounted expeditions to Wawat to obtain timber for shipbuilding and recruits for the Egyptian armies. Since the inhabitants of these regions posed a potential threat to the security of expeditions, the Egyptians tried to maintain good relations with the chiefs, though con-

flict did occasionally take place. In the late Sixth Dynasty, Pepinakht, governor of Aswan, raided Wawat and Irtjet and brought many prisoners away.

During the Sixth Dynasty some rudimentary political development seems to have occurred in Lower Nubia. The autobiography of Harkhuf, governor of Aswan, reveals that about the time of the Egyptian king Merenre, Wawat, Irtjet and Satju all came under the rule of one man. This may even have led to the existence of a short-lived monarchy in northern Nubia; rock-inscriptions of this period attest local rulers who adopted Egyptian-style royal titularies, but were certainly not Egyptian kings. It has been suggested that Lower Nubia was on the verge of becoming a state at this time, but the material culture of the C-Group does not suggest that a significant level of social stratification had yet been attained, and it is likely that political development in the region was intermittent.

Egyptian records of the Sixth Dynasty show that the main goal of expeditions at this time was a region known as the Land of Yam, which lay to the south of Wawat, Irtjet and Satju. Harkhuf made four journeys there, using donkey caravans to avoid the laborious portages which would have been necessary to get boats past the Second Cataract. The account of the products he brought back, which included ebony, incense, oil, leopard-skins, elephant-tusks and throwsticks, show that he was making contact with the African luxury trade. These goods were highly valued, but far more interesting to Harkhuf's master, King Pepy II, was a dancing dwarf which the intrepid governor had acquired on his fourth expedition. In a letter from the court, which Harkhuf proudly had inscribed on the façade of his tomb, the boy-king charged him to take every precaution to ensure that the dwarf arrived safely at Memphis, adding 'My Majesty desires to see this dwarf more than the products of Sinai or of Punt!' Punt, a land of indeterminate origin thought to be near the Red Sea coast, supplied Egypt from time to time with a wide range of exotic products.

Harkhuf's descriptions make it clear that Yam was ruled by a powerful chieftain who controlled the traffic in trade goods arriving from the south and west. The Egyptians were probably only one among many peoples who obtained permission to participate in this trade, and their donkeys doubtless brought presents for the ruler before being loaded with goods for the return trip. The power of this ruler commanded respect in Lower Nubia; the presence of a Yamite escort with Harkhuf's men on one return journey guaranteed him good treatment by the northerners.

It is generally believed, on the grounds of calculations based on the length of Harkhuf's journeys (each one took seven to eight months), and details of the goods he obtained, that Yam lay in the Dongola Reach and that its ruler resided at the site of Kerma. Excavation revealed that a very advanced indigenous culture flourished at the site as early as the twenty-fifth century BC. The rise of this culture to produce one of the first urbanised states in Africa will be described in the next chapter.

3 Egyptian Domination and the Kingdom of Kush

During the First Intermediate Period (c.2181–1991 BC) political instability apparently prevented Egypt from continuing her lucrative contact with the lands to the south. Trade with Yam probably ceased after the Sixth Dynasty, and imported goods such as ivory and ebony become rare in Egyptian graves. As at other times Nubia profited by Egypt's weakness, and both the C-Group population in Lower Nubia and the Kerma Culture to the south developed without disruption.

Passage into Egypt was relatively easy for Nubians at this time and many, no doubt attracted by the prospect of a richer lifestyle, travelled north and sold their services as mercenaries, playing a conspicuous role in the civil wars which led ultimately to the reunification of Egypt. These included C-Group people from Wawat, Medjay from the Eastern Desert, and perhaps also men from the Kerma region. A well-known model of a troop of Nubian archers, found in a tomb of this period at Asyut, shows careful observation on the craftsman's part of the distinctive hairstyle, dark brown skin-colour and ornamental leather loincloths which typified the southerners. Graves and settlements show that some of these Nubians settled in Upper Egypt, but others returned home, taking with them to the grave Egyptian objects perhaps brought back from their service in the north.

By the beginning of the second millennium BC Egypt was reunited and had entered upon the period of strength and prosperity known as the Middle Kingdom. Her rulers were thus once more in a position to exploit the resources and trading networks of the south as their ancestors had done. Aware also of the potential threat to their security from the growing power in the Kerma Basin, the Egyptian kings aimed to conquer and annex the whole of Lower Nubia and achieved this mainly through the efforts of the Twelfth Dynasty kings Senusret I and Senusret III, who 15 launched a series of military campaigns to break local resistance and established a new frontier of Egyptian control at Semna, south of the Second Cataract.

To protect the new frontier and to administer and exploit the region a chain of massive mud-brick fortresses was constructed at stra- 16 tegic points along the Nile. Situated on river banks and on islands no two were identical in design, the plan and construction being adapted to the local terrain. Their elaborate defensive systems reflect an exceptionally high standard of military architecture and include several devices not otherwise known until the medieval period. Standard features were huge enclosure walls, ramparts and ditches, bastions and massive fortified gates with drawbridges. Inside were administrative quarters, storerooms and barracks, workshops and small temples dedicated to Egyptian gods. The

15 Stela of Senusret III from Elephantine. Below the king's names and titles is an inscription recording building work at the fortress of Elephantine which the king ordered to be done at the time of a military expedition against Kush. H. 37 cm.

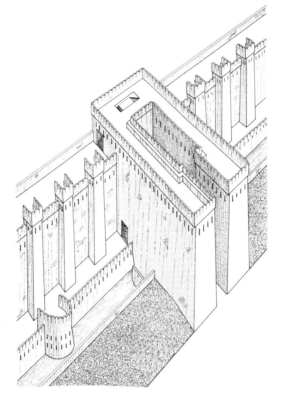

16 Reconstruction of the West Gate of the fortress of Buhen on the opposite bank to Wadi Halfa. This was one of the best-preserved of the series of military installations erected by the Egyptian kings of the Twelfth Dynasty to control the conquered territory of Lower Nubia.

17 Head of a black-granite statue of King Senusret III from Deir el-Bahri, Thebes. In his reign Egyptian control of Nubia was extended as far south as Semna, upstream of the Second Cataract.

disposition of the defences at large fortresses such as Buhen indicates that they were intended to fend off attacks from the desert, as well as from the south. Indeed, the menace of desert nomads such as the Medjay may at first have posed a greater threat to the security of the area than did the Kerma people to the south. The forts were manned by garrisons of Egyptian troops, perhaps numbering as many as a thousand in a large installation such as Buhen. The garrisons were regularly relieved and kept well-supplied with rations and other essentials by river.

The main concentration of military installations was at the Semna Gorge. The narrowness and the rocky bed of the Nile here made this spot easily defensible, and Senusret III 17 turned it into an impregnable barrier, erecting a pair of fortresses on the rocky bluffs of Semna and Kumma, another on the island of Uronarti immediately to the north, and perhaps also a great stone dam across the river, leaving only a single narrow channel for boats to pass through.

The role of the fortresses was as much economic as it was defensive. They controlled all trade and traffic moving north, not only by river but along the desert roads as well. No Nubian was permitted to pass north of the Second Cataract except to trade with the Egyptians, and all goods destined for Egypt were collected at the fortress of Mirgissa, where they were loaded on to ships for transport. Besides trade goods, the fortresses also received the fruits of Egyptian exploitation of local mineral resources. In the reign of Senusret I the gold mines in the Wadi el-Allaqi and its tributary the Wadi Gabgaba, running east from the Nile between the First and Second Cataracts, began to be worked. Copper was mined at Abu Seyal, and the diorite quarries in the desert west of Toshka were reopened. The fortress of Quban, at the mouth of the Wadi el-Allaqi, became the base for the mining operations and most of the gold was smelted and stored there. The finding of scales and weights for weighing gold at Semna and Uronarti indicates that expeditions beyond the frontier were sometimes made to tap the more easily extractable gold deposits along the Nile south of the Second Cataract.

The system instituted by the Twelfth Dynasty kings operated successfully for about two hundred years, and the fortresses seem never to have been captured. This was due not only to the sophistication of their fortifications, but also to the careful surveillance maintained over all indigenous activity, even when involving quite small groups of individuals. A unique and valuable papyrus archive discovered in Egypt gives an insight into the day-to-day activities of the fortress garrisons in the Thirteenth Dynasty. The documents are the dispatches sent by officers in charge of several fortresses, including Semna, to a superior in Egypt, describing trading with the local Nubians and the sending out of desert patrols to watch the movements of potentially troublesome groups such as the Medjay.

In contrast to the nomads, who were clearly unpredictable and needed to be watched, the settled C-Group population of Lower Nubia seems to have coexisted fairly amicably with the occupying Egyptians. They were not, apparently, heavily exploited and, benefitting from the peaceful conditions imposed by the conquerors, their numbers increased. Major existing settlements such as those at Aniba and Faras continued to flourish, and new ones were founded. C-Group people often dwelt near the fortresses but although they traded with the Egyptians there was no significant cultural interaction, and the native inhabitants probably continued to follow their traditional lifestyle, cultivating the narrow floodplain and herding cattle. Since the Egyptians no longer needed to purchase the co-operation of the C-Group, trade between them declined.

Culturally, development was steady, if slow. Larger and better-built houses, partly of stone, were erected and graves were more carefully constructed, the burial pit sometimes having a stone lining. Black-topped red ware and incised black ware continued as the standard ceramic products. The latter pots show an evolution from a round- to a flat-bottomed type with the rim drawn inwards, and a few new types of vessel appeared, notably globular pots of coarse red ware with scratched geometric and figured decoration. Pottery models of women and cattle occur in graves, but otherwise gifts for the dead were simple: leather garments and sandals, and locally made jewellery of bone, shell, faience and stone. A few graves contained bronze mirrors but other metal objects were rare, particularly weapons, which the Egyptians may have been reluctant to trade with the C-Group.

Although the C-Group enjoyed increased prosperity in this period their society did not advance politically. Houses and graves show little of the differentiation which might suggest

18 Part of a hieratic papyrus from Thebes containing dispatches sent from the commanders of several fortresses in Lower Nubia, describing contact with the local population and the tracking by Egyptian garrison troops of groups of Medjay nomads. H. 16 cm.

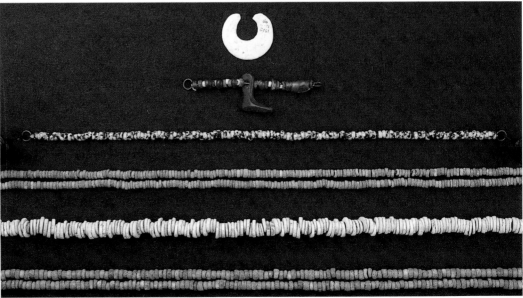

19 (*Above*) C-Group pottery from the cemetery at Faras. The pieces all date to the early second millennium BC and include bowls of polished incised ware and a jar of coarse redware.

20 (*Right*) Necklaces and a foot-shaped pendant from C-Group graves of the early second millennium BC at Faras.

the emergence of a hierarchical society. This, together with their apparent cultural isolation, may reflect an Egyptian policy of restricting contacts between the C-Group and the more advanced Kerma Culture to the south in order to hold back political development.

It was to the region in which this Kerma Culture flourished that the Egyptians of the early second millennium BC began to apply the name Kush. The modern term for the culture is derived from Kerma, an archaeological site of unrivalled importance in the Dongola Reach. As mentioned previously, this was probably the 'Land of Yam' to which Egyptian traders journeyed at the end of the Old Kingdom, and Harkhuf's autobiography suggests that it was even then a highly organised chiefdom, the ruler of which controlled the northward passage of trade goods from central and northeast Africa. Excavations at the cemeteries of Kerma initially by Reisner and more recently by the Swiss Archaeological Mission indicate that a high degree of social stratification already existed in the late third millennium BC. By the time of the Egyptian occupation of Lower Nubia, it was the capital of the first important African state outside Egypt.

The measures taken by the Egyptians to protect their southern frontier and to turn Lower Nubia into a buffer zone packed with troops are an eloquent testimony to the strength of the Kushites and the seriousness of the threat they posed. Originally, the Egyptian kings' intention had probably been to extend their frontier beyond Semna and gain direct control of the African luxury trade, but although they had campaigned against Kush this evidently proved too great a task. On a pair of boundary stelae erected in his sixteenth regnal year Senusret III boasts of his victories over the southerners, contemptuously dismissing his foes as craven-hearted wretches, unworthy of respect. But alongside the bombastic phrases there is a warning to future

kings that perpetual vigilance is necessary at the southern boundary if Egypt's position is to be maintained.

The origins of the Kerma Culture are still imperfectly understood, but there is no doubt that the A- and C-Group cultures and those of the Eastern Desert, the Sahara and the Upper Nile region were all among the formative influences. At the height of its development, as the 'Kingdom of Kush', in the seventeenth and early sixteenth centuries BC, its advanced status is marked not only by the existence of a hierarchical society headed by a king, but by its stability and the creation within its territory of monumental structures, requiring the efficient organisation of a substantial labour-force.

The strategic location of Kerma in one of the most fertile stretches of the Nubian Nile valley was probably an important factor in the kingdom's prosperity. Agriculture and animal husbandry flourished and formed the backbone of the economy, but perhaps more important were the profits gained by the rulers as a result of their fortunate position as middlemen on the great African trade routes. Ivory, ebony and other southern luxuries were reaching Egypt again in quantity via Nubia, despite the occasional hostilities between the two lands, and the abundance of Egyptian objects found at Kerma (the presence of which contributed to earlier, erroneous interpretations of the site as an Egyptian trading colony) indicates that this trade was reciprocal.

The ancient town of Kerma, was one of the earliest urbanised communities in tropical Africa. A settlement existed at the site from the late fourth millennium BC, but the main town began its growth c.2400 BC, and remained in continuous occupation for a thousand years. Its central nucleus was a massive structure of unbaked brick, now known as the Western 'Deffufa' (a local term for any large brick building). It appears to have been the principal

religious building of Kerma, and comprised a large tower-like structure linked to a rectangular block, with gently sloping undecorated walls. The general shape is reminiscent of that of an Egyptian temple with a pylon gateway, and some of the building techniques used suggest that the prototype may have been some now-vanished type of brick edifice of contemporary Egypt. The Deffufa was one of the oldest buildings at Kerma and underwent considerable alteration before reaching its final form, by which time it was an almost solid block of masonry. Inside there was only a narrow central passage, apparently the sanctuary, and a staircase leading to the flat roof. What took place there is unknown. A limestone slab found in front of the sanctuary may have served as a sacrificial altar, while other ceremonies may have been conducted on the roof-terrace.

In the 'Classic' phase of Kerma's development (c.1750–1600 BC) the Deffufa stood with workshops and other religious buildings within an enclosed precinct which seems to have constituted a 'religious quarter'. To the south-west stood a large circular hut constructed of wood and brick, clearly another important building as it was maintained over a long period and enlarged several times. Its function is unknown but analogies from more recent periods of Sudanese history suggest that it may have served as a royal audience hall. The main streets and houses of the inhabitants were grouped haphazardly around these two focal points. The dwellings varied in size from one-roomed huts to relatively luxurious structures not unlike modern Nubian houses, with two or three rooms and a walled courtyard containing animal pens and granaries. Evidence of the turbulent history of

21 The Western Deffufa at Kerma. This monumental brick structure was the principal religious building in the capital of the Nubian kingdom of Kush.

Kerma is provided by the dry ditches and massive mud-brick walls which protected the town and which were repeatedly rebuilt as the settlement expanded. Destruction levels with clear traces of burning bear witness to the fact that the town was burnt down and afterwards rebuilt on several occasions.

This advanced level of urbanisation was accompanied by a high standard of craftsmanship. Among the skills most fully developed by the Kerma artisans was that of working bronze, and excellent daggers, tools and toilet articles were produced in this medium. A bronze foundry, excavated in 1980, yielded a well-preserved rectangular kiln, parts of crucibles and traces of metal, but no slag, indicating that those employed here were engaged in the manufacture of finished products. The foundry was situated close to the Deffufa, within the religious enclosure at the centre of the town, suggesting that at Kerma, as in Egypt at some periods, the production of metalwork was controlled by the temples. The same may be true of the manufacture of faience, another craft in which the Kushites were adept. Some of the brick funerary chapels in the cemetery of Kerma were decorated with brilliant blue faience tiles in the shape of animals, plants and protective symbols. Vases of faience were common and human figurines

in the same material have been found.

Attractive jewellery was made from gold, silver, semi-precious stones, faience, ivory and ostrich-eggshell. Ivory, and occasionally bronze, was also used to produce bird- and animal-shaped inlays to decorate the headboards of wooden beds which usually had legs carved to look like those of animals and were themselves superb examples of carpentry and joinery. Other ornaments in the shape of birds, lions and giraffes were made from mica, to be sewn on to leather caps worn by sacrificial victims buried in the graves of some of the Kushite rulers.

The most characteristic products of the Kerma craftsmen, however, are the ceramics which, at their finest, represent one of the highest peaks of African achievement in this field. During the Classic phase of the culture large numbers of 'tulip'-shaped beakers, round-bottomed with an elegant flaring rim, were produced. Though handmade, they have extremely thin walls and a pleasing regularity of form. The colour scheme is equally distinctive: an irregular silver-grey band separates the glossy red-brown of the lower part from the burnished black of the lip and the interior. The beakers display a remarkable uniformity of shape, though a small number are varied by the addition of a long upwardly-angled spout.

The majority of the finest Kerma pottery is found in graves and it is these above all else which testify most plainly to the kingdom's growing wealth and independence. Graves became increasingly elaborate and the burial goods more numerous and of progressively better quality. The standard grave type was the earth tumulus with a burial pit beneath. The body, dressed in leather garments, sandals and jewellery, was often laid on a bed. Since the Kushites had no written language, the nature of their beliefs about the afterlife can only be conjectured, but care was clearly taken to provide basic necessities for the dead.

22, 23 Bronze dagger (above) and razors (right) from Kerma. Technologically these pieces compare favourably with contemporary Egyptian examples but the shapes are distinctive of the Kerma Culture. The high standard achieved by the craftsmen was in part due to the use of an advanced type of kiln which could be heated to a very high temperature. Classic Kerma phase, c.1750–1600 BC. L. of dagger 49 cm; L. of razors 16.2 and 16.9 cm.

24 'Tulip' beaker of the Classic Kerma phase. Large quantities of this fine pottery have been found in graves at Kerma and at other sites in Upper Nubia. H. 11.8 cm.

injuries found on the skeletons, and by the regular burying of weapons with the dead. One of the most striking discoveries made at Kerma was the well-preserved burial of a young archer of the Early phase (c.2500– 25 2050 BC). He lay on his side, his bow and bowstring at his right hand, as if ready to leap up and fight at a moment's notice. A fillet around his head held in place a tall feather, a fashion which typifies the Nubians in Egyptian and Assyrian representations. A typical 54 funerary practice found in many of the earlier Kerma burials, including this one, is the placing of the body on a tanned ox-hide, with another laid over the top. Cattle, besides being of economic importance, and hence a status symbol, possessed religious significance for early Nubian societies and their skulls and horns are often found in association with burials. This custom reached its height in the Kerma cemeteries, where hundreds of ox-skulls were arranged around the southern edge of several of the larger tumuli.

If the slaughtering of large numbers of cattle at a funeral was one indication of the importance of the deceased, the size of the grave mound and the opulence of the contents were others. The richest graves of all were those of the last kings of Kush, who ruled the kingdom in the late seventeenth and early sixteenth centuries BC. Their massive tumuli, with large brick funerary chapels nearby, yielded some surprising finds when they were excavated by G. A. Reisner in 1913–14. The principal burial lay on a bed in a small chamber beneath the mound. In the largest mounds there was an internal framework of mud-brick walls arranged on either side of a broad central corridor in which were buried hundreds of men, women and children, all of whom had apparently been sacrificed at the ruler's funeral. The 'sacrificial corridor' of Tumulus X, one of the largest sepulchres, 26 contained over three hundred such victims,

The inverted bowls discovered around many graves perhaps represent the remains of a funeral meal shared between the mourners and the deceased. More food offerings were placed inside the graves and sheep were often sacrificed and buried with the corpse. The presence of horn-ornaments and an ostrich-feather disc on the heads of several of these animals probably indicates that some religious significance was attached to them. In the later phases of the kingdom's history the sheep-sacrifices were gradually replaced by those of humans, perhaps servants of the deceased who were killed to accompany their master into the next life.

The contents of the graves also emphasise the strong warlike tradition of the Kerma people, both by the frequent ante-mortem

25 Burial of a young archer in the cemetery at Kerma. The body lay on an ox-hide and was accompanied by weapons and other gifts. Early Kerma phase, c.2500–2050 BC.

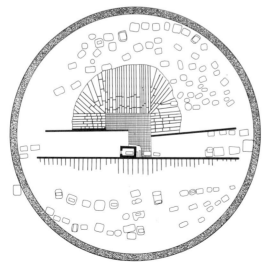

26 Plan of Tumulus x at Kerma, the grave of one of the last rulers of Kush. The small rectangular chamber in the centre contained the principal burial. In the long transverse passage were discovered the skeletons' of hundreds of retainers ceremonially put to death at the ruler's funeral.

the majority of whom were women – perhaps members of the ruler's harem. Surprisingly, this custom of retainer sacrifice in the Kushite kingdom appears to have increased as the state prospered and as the culture grew more sophisticated, in contrast to developments in Egypt and Mesopotamia.

The kingdom had reached the peak of its development by the late seventeenth century BC. The Egyptians were forced to withdraw their forces from Lower Nubia, due to internal weakness and the Hyksos takeover of the Delta region, leaving a power-vacuum which the Kushites quickly filled. Extending their control northward, they captured the fortresses at the Second Cataract and occupied a number of strategic sites as far north as Aswan. A remnant of the Egyptian garrisons had continued to occupy the main fortresses and their associated settlements and, as there was now no possibility of being replaced by relief troops, they made Lower Nubia their permanent home, intermarrying with the local population and opting to be buried at the fortresses when they died. Some of these Egyptians found no difficulty in transferring their allegience to the new rulers: Sepedher, Commander of Buhen, even built a temple to Horus on behalf of the Ruler of Kush.

Kushite control of the southern trade routes was now at its strongest and the kingdom was able to trade with Egypt on unusually favourable terms, as the preponderance of imports obtained from Upper Egypt at this time indicates. The subject C-Group people in the north of Nubia probably also benefited from this situation, receiving substantial quantities of imported Egyptian goods and at the same time enjoying a marked advance in culture, which is apparent in the greater elaboration of houses and tombs, and a diversification in pottery and other goods. The turbulent events of these times are, however, reflected in the appearance of fortified C-Group settlements at Areika and Wadi es-Sebua. Politically, though, the C-Group never achieved the advanced status of Kush.

A conspicuous element in the populations of Egypt and Nubia at this date were nomadic groups, of which the Medjay are the best known. At various times during the third and second millennia BC bands of these people descended from their homeland in the Eastern Desert into the Nile valley, where they regularly found employment as soldiers in the Egyptian armies, often serving in a special capacity as desert scouts. On account of the simple tribal nature of their society, however, the allegiance of individual groups was narrow, and Egyptians who ventured up the Wadi el-Allaqi to mine gold were likely to meet with hostility from the local Medjay people there.

Identification of the material culture of the Medjay poses problems. Another nomadic Nubian group, the 'Pan-Grave' people, entered southern Egypt and northern Nubia in considerable numbers during the late Middle Kingdom and Second Intermediate Period, but did not rapidly become integrated into local societies. Although their cultural identity, as reconstructed from grave goods, fits with what is known of the Medjay it is not certain that they are one and the same people. The Pan-Grave Nubians take their name from the distinctive shallow circular pits in which they were buried. Their pottery includes incised ware and black-topped red ware vessels, and shows links not only with the ceramics of the C-Group and the Kerma Culture but also, and perhaps more significantly, with that of groups from the Eastern Desert and the Gash Delta near the Red Sea coast.

The Pan-Grave people were physically robust, wore kilts of leather and ornaments and jewellery made from shells (notably varieties peculiar to the Red Sea), faience and ostrich-eggshell. Bracelets made of mother-of-pearl

27 (*Above*) Black-topped redware pot from a Pan-Grave at Mostagedda. H. 8.2 cm.

28 Battle-axe with its original wooden handle. The blade is incised with the cartouche of the otherwise unattested Egyptian king Nebmaatre of the late Second Intermediate Period (c.1786–1550 BC). From a Pan-Grave at Mostagedda. L. 41 cm.

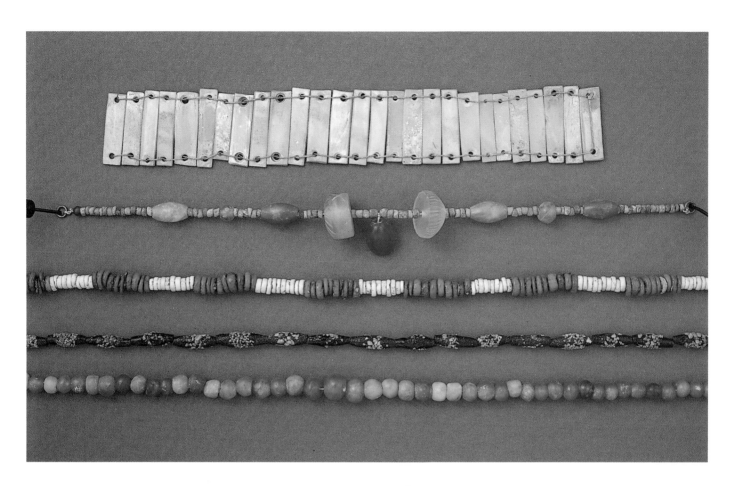

29 Jewellery from a Pan-Grave cemetery at Mostagedda, including a bracelet of mother-of-pearl plaques and necklaces of faience, shell, cornelian and other semi-precious stones. L. of mother-of-pearl bracelet 17 cm.

plaques are among the most characteristic finds in their cemeteries, and they also followed the typically Nubian custom of burying skulls and horns of oxen, sheep and gazelles, sometimes painted with patterns, in their graves. One skull from a grave at Mostagedda in Upper Egypt carries a unique depiction of a Pan-Grave chief, whose name is written before

him in Egyptian hieroglyphs. He grasps a throwstick, and a battle axe is slung across his shoulder. Axes of exactly this type are found in several of the Pan-graves, together with other weapons and archery equipment – significant in view of the events which were shortly to change the political map of north-east Africa so dramatically.

28

4 Nubia in the Egyptian New Kingdom

In the mid-sixteenth century BC Egypt recovered from the weakness of the Second Intermediate Period, thanks to the efforts of the Theban rulers who liberated the country from the domination of the Hyksos and strengthened the frontiers. Carried on by the momentum of these successes, they went on to extend their control over the lands to the north-east and to the south, creating a foreign empire which brought immense wealth to Egypt and made her one of the greatest powers in the Near East.

King Kamose, in whose reign the struggle began in earnest, was faced with enemies both to the north and to the south of his small Upper Egyptian state. The Hyksos rulers controlled all of Egypt from the Delta almost to Asyut, and the Ruler of Kush exercised control over the whole of Nubia as far north as Aswan. In about 1560 BC the Hyksos ruler Aaweserre Apophis attempted to forge an alliance with the Kushite king so as to crush the Theban kingdom by forcing Kamose to fight simultaneously on two fronts. This move failed after the messenger carrying Apophis' letter was captured by the Egyptians as he made his way to Kush by the oasis route. Kamose launched military offensives against both lands, and his achievements were continued by his successor Ahmose I, founder of the New Kingdom, who expelled the Hyksos from Egypt and began the reconquest of Lower Nubia.

During the reigns of Ahmose and his son Amenhotep I the Egyptian armies gradually pushed southward. The Second Cataract fortresses were recaptured, and at Buhen the fortifications were repaired. This area became a buffer zone, but only temporarily, for Ahmose's troops advanced further south, at least as far as the island of Sai, an important Kushite settlement at the northern end of the Dongola Reach.

Against this background of Egyptian hostility towards Nubia, contact between the inhabitants of the two lands continued unabated. Both Kushite and Medjay Nubians had served in the Egyptian army during the 'war of liberation', and were to continue to do so throughout the New Kingdom. Some Kushites may have moved to the north of Egypt after the expulsion of the Hyksos, as Kerma artifacts of very late type have been found as far north as Saqqara. A man buried there perhaps in about the reign of Amenhotep I was accompanied by a variety of goods including two 'tulip' beakers of Kerma type but inferior manufacture, several fine faience vessels and pieces of jewellery, and a Cypriot Base Ring ware juglet.

During the early stages of the Egyptian reconquest of Nubia the Kushites seem to have offered little effective opposition, but the heart

30 Stela dated to the eighth year of the reign of Amenhotep I, found reused at Qasr Ibrim. The scene depicts the king with two queens, both identified as queen Ahmose Nefertary, offering to the god Horus, lord of Miam. H. 1.14 m.

31 Pottery and faience vessels from the grave of a man at Saqqara. The group includes Egyptian pieces as well as foreign imports such as the Cypriot Base Ring jug. The small beakers of Kerma type are of inferior manufacture and lack the distinctive grey-white band separating the black top from the red body. The faience cup and rhyton (drinking cup) are probably also of Nubian manufacture. H. of tallest vessel 27 cm.

of their kingdom remained intact until the accession to the Egyptian throne of Thutmose I. In a major campaign launched in his second year, he broke the power of Kush. Their army was defeated in battle and the ruler was killed. Kerma itself probably fell, and the signs of burning and destruction found during excavations suggest that the town was sacked by the Egyptians on this occasion. The massive outer defences were demolished, perhaps in an effort to prevent the place being refortified as a centre of resistance. Thutmose I, besides garrisoning Sai and Tombos, apparently penetrated as far as Kurgus, beyond the Fourth Cataract, before returning to Egypt with the dead body of the defeated Kushite leader displayed at the prow of his ship as a grim warning.

This campaign marked the turning-point in the Egyptians' attempts to overcome Kush, but the southerners were not yet vanquished. During the next half-century Egyptian armies had to quell numerous rebellions, from which they brought away many prisoners. Kerma continued to be occupied by Kushites and may

still have been a thorn in Egypt's side until the pacification of Nubia was completed by Thutmose III. Early in his reign, while he shared the throne with Queen Hatshepsut, campaigns against Nubia took place, his intention probably being to secure Egypt's southern boundary before he embarked on his ambitious conquest of Syria-Palestine. The region of the Fourth Cataract, a natural boundary which was known as Karoy, was chosen as the new frontier, and all the territory north to Aswan was permanently annexed, though looser control was probably exerted over the area between the Fourth and Fifth Cataracts. The frontier settlement of Napata was built close to Gebel Barkal, a great flat-topped butte which was the most striking landmark in the area.

By the end of Thutmose III's reign Egypt had secured substantial imperial possessions in the Levant as well as in Nubia. Both regions were intensively exploited but the manner of their treatment was different. The provinces of Syria-Palestine were controlled by Egyptian governors, under whose authority the rulers

32 (*Right*) Right-hand portion of a painted limestone stela dated to the thirty-fifth year of the reign of King Thutmose III, who appears wearing the Blue Crown and stands before a deity whose figure is lost. Obtained from Wadi Halfa, the piece was probably originally set up at Buhen. H. 61 cm.

33 (*Below*) Relief from the Temple of Armant in Upper Egypt showing a horned animal, probably a rhinoceros, presented to Thutmose III together with other produce of Nubia. Although the rhinoceros was rarely seen by the Egyptians, Thutmose III is known to have shot or captured one during a Nubian expedition.

of minor states and cities were allowed to retain their positions, as vassals of the pharaoh, and to run the day-to-day affairs of their territories much as they had always done. In Nubia, however, an Egyptian imperial government was imposed to oversee the administration of the land at every level.

At the head of the civil administration was the viceroy, who acted as the pharaoh's deputy. He was appointed directly by the Egyptian king and usually bore the titles 'Overseer of the Southern Lands' and 'King's Son of Kush'. His main duties were the running of the administration of Nubia, and the exploitation and collection of the valuable resources obtained from Nubia itself and from the south. He also organised building work on the king's behalf and was responsible for military operations in the region.

The administration was based on the system operating in Egypt. The new territory was subdivided into a northern and a southern province, respectively named Wawat and Kush, the government of which was in the hands of two deputies. In addition, there were other minor officials including stewards, administrators and scribes. Several smaller territorial divisions existed and these were ruled by native chiefs, though their authority did not equal that wielded by the Palestinian vassals.

Besides organising the exploitation of the gold mines and forwarding the proceeds to the treasuries in Egypt, the viceroy also received the products of central Africa entering Egyptian territory at Napata. His position was thus one of exceptional power, and implied great trust on the part of the king, for besides having control of a major part of Egypt's wealth he could also call on extensive reserves of manpower and was entitled to command his own troops, although the soldiers stationed in Nubia were normally under the control of the 'Battalion Commander of Kush'. These factors,

34 Gebel Barkal, the flat-topped 'Holy Mountain' near which the Egyptian frontier settlement of Napata was located. The mountain was believed to be the dwelling place of the local form of the god Amen-Re, and several temples were erected there in his honour.

35 (*Right*) Lower half of a sandstone statue of Ahmose, also called Turi, the best documented of the early Egyptian viceroys of Nubia. Turi began his career as a temple scribe and was promoted to be Commander of Buhen before rising to the office of Viceroy in the reign of Amenhotep I. H. 48 cm.

36 (*Far right*) One of the most active Egyptian viceroys in the reign of Ramesses II was Setau. He constructed the temples of Gerf Husein and Wadi es-Sebua on behalf of his master and left inscriptions throughout Nubia commemorating his deeds. On this relief from Buhen he is depicted pouring a libation before the Egyptian goddess Renenutet. H. 50 cm.

together with the ease of access to Egypt, meant that the security of the kingdom was to some extent dependent on the loyalty of the viceroy. Fortunately no viceroy seems to have successfully taken advantage of his position until the Egyptian domination of Nubia broke down at the end of the New Kingdom.

The gold mines were now intensively worked. Inscriptions from the Eighteenth Dynasty record large quantities of precious metal received, subdivided into 'Gold of Wawat' and 'Gold of Kush', and wall-paintings in the tomb chapels of some Theban officials include scenes of Nubians presenting gold to the king. The extent to which the Egyptians identified Nubia with its most desirable product is reflected in one of the viceroy's secondary titles, 'Overseer of the Gold Lands of the Lord of the Two Lands'. The richest deposits, the Gold of Wawat, came from the Wadi el-Allaqi mines, which were now being exploited more intensively than ever before. In the course of the New Kingdom, however, attempts were made to extend mining operations to other areas. This seems to have been a direct consequence of the development of diplomatic relations between Egypt and other powers in the Near East in the Eighteenth Dynasty. Gold was the resource which foreign potentates most wanted from Egypt and it became a vital bargaining counter in international diplomacy. In the reign of Amenhotep III the Viceroy Merymose and other officials commanded a series of military expeditions in the area of the Eastern Desert, probably to prepare the way for the opening of new mining areas. Some of the regions which began to be worked at this time, such as Ibhet and Ikayta, remained important sources of gold until the last years of the New Kingdom. The region was notoriously inhospitable and several kings had to send armies against the local inhabitants who were attacking the miners. The water supply was also a problem and Sety I and Ramesses II sunk wells to save their miners from dying of thirst in the burning heat of the desert wadis. Even then the conditions under which miners worked in the Eastern Desert remained appalling. An inscription recording a 9,000 strong mission sent to the Wadi Hammamat in the reign of Ramesses IV casually mentions that nine hundred persons perished in the course of the expedition.

The Nile trade route to the African interior was now controlled directly by the Egyptians for the first time. An annual ceremony took place at which the viceroy presented to the pharaoh the fruits of the exploitation of Nubia, viewed through Egyptian eyes as 'tribute'. This event was depicted on the walls of several Theban tomb chapels and a similar presentation scene was carved in the rock-temple of Ramesses II at Beit el-Wali. The scenes provide a comprehensive account of the produce obtained from and via the southlands. Besides the familiar gold, leopard-skins, elephant-tusks, ebony logs, and ostrich-eggs and -feathers, there is a variety of exotic live animals: lions, antelopes, ostriches, gazelles, giraffes, monkeys and leopards.

Several Nubians are also included, shown as bound prisoners, a reminder of the fact that some of the inhabitants were sent to Egypt as slaves. These people might be employed as labourers on religious and civil establishments, while others served as a police force, and large numbers were recruited into the Egyptian army, usually destined for service in the Levant, where their undisciplined behaviour sometimes made them unpopular. A letter, found in the Amarna archive, from Abdiheba, ruler of Jerusalem, describes how unruly Nubian troops belonging to the king of Egypt had broken through the roof of his palace and nearly killed him.

For those Nubians who remained at home, conditions may not have been much better. The Egyptians displayed little respect for the

37 Painted cast of scenes on a wall in the temple of Beit el-Wali, the first of a series constructed in Nubia by Ramesses II. The Viceroy Amenemope is rewarded with gold collars (top) while ebony logs, ivory tusks, ostrich eggs, feathers, gold, furniture and weapons are presented to the pharaoh. At the bottom are captives and other Nubians bringing a giraffe, a gazelle, monkeys and a leopard.

indigenous way of life and pursued a deliberate policy of acculturation, attempting to break down the ethnic identity of the Nubians by forcing them to adopt Egyptian manners and customs in a way never attempted on the same scale in the Levantine provinces. The native Nubian chiefs who controlled the smaller districts seem to have set an example for their subjects to follow. Their sons were taken to Egypt as hostages and educated at the court, where they were taught the Egyptian language, given Egyptian names, and persuaded to adopt Egyptian dress and customs. They were then sent back to be rulers of their local chiefdoms, very much in the manner of native officials in the British colonial system in India three thousand years later. Small 'dynasties' of these Egyptianised chiefs can be identified in some areas of Lower Nubia. Chiefs like Djehutyhotep and Amenemhat, rulers of the province of Tehkhet, and Heqanefer, prince of Miam, were buried according to the customs of their overlords, in rock-cut tombs with wall-paintings of Egyptian type accompanied by hieroglyphic inscriptions, and they adopted the use of *shabti* figures (small human figurines to act as servants in the afterlife).

One of the roles of these chiefs may have

been to promote the acculturation of the indigenous population. In some areas this seems to have been achieved thoroughly, and manifestations of the C-Group culture virtually disappeared in Lower Nubia, to be replaced by houses, graves and manufactures copying Egyptian models. In other areas Egyptian culture seems to have been resisted and native burial customs were retained. The blanket of Egyptian culture which spread over much of Nubia makes it hard to discover the lifestyle of the indigenous inhabitants in this period, and it must be conjectured that they continued to subsist by mixed farming, much as before.

The Egyptian domination of Nubia left its mark on the land even more emphatically in the shape of numerous monumental buildings. With the establishing of the frontier at Napata the fortresses in the Second Cataract area became redundant as defences. Some of the more important, such as Quban, Aniba, Serra and Buhen, were renovated and served as centres of administration, commerce and mining operations, but the others received little attention. During the second half of the Eighteenth Dynasty towns and temples superseded the forts as the main manifestations

38 (*Left*) Wall painting in the tomb chapel of Huy at Thebes, showing Heqanefer, Prince of Miam, and other Nubian chiefs bowing before King Tutankhamun. Though his features proclaim him a Nubian, Heqanefer was one of a number of local rulers who adopted Egyptian dress and customs in the New Kingdom. (Copy by Nina Davies.)

39 (*Right*) Faience vessel decorated with blue lotuses, from the Egyptian town at Sesebi in Upper Nubia. An almost identical specimen is in the Metropolitan Museum of Art, New York. H. 14.5 cm.

of the imperial presence. This development involved the renovation of old-established settlements and the foundation of new ones, such as the towns at Amara West and Sesebi. Though walled, military defensibility was not a priority in the layout of these towns, and a stone temple was the most prominent feature. Centres such as Aniba and Amara served periodically as the viceroy's residence, and these as well as other settlements such as Faras were major centres of occupation by administrators, miners, and military personnel.

The building of temples in Nubia increased dramatically during the Eighteenth and Nineteenth Dynasties. The early Eighteenth Dynasty temples were mainly situated within the Second Cataract forts and were relatively simple affairs of mud-brick and local sandstone. The most important religious site in Nubia in the New Kingdom was Gebel Barkal, near to Napata. This spot, called the 'Holy Mountain' by the Egyptians, became the Nubian centre of the cult of Amun, the state god of Egypt, and the first of many temples was built at its foot in the Eighteenth Dynasty.

During the reign of Amenhotep III two other impressive temples were erected at the remote Upper Nubian sites of Soleb and Sedeinga, the former dedicated to the worship of Amenhotep himself and the latter to his consort, Queen Tiye (a memory of whose name may survive in one of the modern names for the site, Adey). A magnificent pair of red granite lions which originally stood at the temple of Soleb are now in the British Museum.

The best-known Egyptian temples in Nubia are the two rock-cut shrines constructed in the reign of Ramesses II at Abu Simbel. These were part of a series of six temples which the king had built along the Nile between Beit el-Wali, south of Aswan, and Aksha, near Faras. While all these structures can be regarded as immense pieces of propaganda, designed to hammer home the message that Ramesses and the gods of Egypt who were his patrons were truly the masters of Nubia, the Abu Simbel temples had a more individual significance as well; in the 'Great Temple' Ramesses appears worshipping not only Amun and Re-Harakhty, but also himself as a divinity, while in the

40 (*Above right*) New Kingdom votive offerings to Hathor from Faras. Hathor was worshipped by miners and others who worked in desert regions. A sanctuary dedicated to her, and founded by Queen Hatshepsut, existed at Faras. These small female figurines represent one category of the numerous objects dedicated there by devotees.

41 (*Right*) Ruins of the temple erected by Amenhotep III at Soleb. (From a drawing made in the mid-nineteenth century by George Alexander Hoskins.)

42 (*Left*) Red granite statue of a recumbent lion, one of a pair originally set up by Amenhotep III at the temple of Soleb. They were discovered at Gebel Barkal, where they had been removed in the third century BC by the Meroitic king Amanislo, who added his name to the statues.

43 (*Below*) Façade of the temple of Ramesses II at Abu Simbel, salvaged and reconstructed as part of the Unesco rescue campaign. This, the largest temple in Nubia, was built by war captives during the early years of the king's reign. One of the four figures of Ramesses on the façade was shattered by an earthquake shortly after the structure was completed.

smaller temple Ramesses' wife, Queen Nefertari, identified with the goddess Hathor, is the main focus of attention.

Despite the intensive activity both in mining and in temple-building during the reign of Ramesses II, the population of Lower Nubia was decreasing significantly. While textual sources indicate that Nubia continued to be governed and exploited well into the Twentieth Dynasty, there is surprisingly little archaeological evidence for the existence of a settled population in the north. The reasons for this apparent depopulation, which seems to have continued throughout the first millennium BC, are unknown. Among the suggested explanations are Egyptian overexploitation of Nubia's human resources, and a long-term fluctuation in the level of the Nile which may have had a sufficiently adverse effect on agricultural productivity to cause the inhabitants to move away in search of a more favourable environment.

The Egyptian domination of Nubia lasted for almost five hundred years. During the last century of the New Kingdom, however, Egyptian activity there declined. The weakening of the central government, corruption in the administration, and the high price of food and raw materials placed tremendous strain on the fabric of society. Most of Egypt's Levantine possessions were lost and her manpower resources were kept busy defending the eastern and northern borders from attack. In the late Nineteenth and Twentieth Dynasties there was a decline in the productivity of the Nubian goldfields, and the consequent decrease in mining and other activities led to the eventual abandonment of the pharaonic settlements and the withdrawal of the provincial administration to Egypt.

The final straw came at the end of the Twentieth Dynasty. Serious civil disturbances broke out in Egypt and the pharaoh Ramesses XI summoned the Viceroy of Nubia, Panehesy, to restore order with troops under his command. Having done so, Panehesy rebelled against the throne. Though he was forced out of Egypt, campaigns to recover Nubia were evidently unsuccessful and the struggle marked the end of Egyptian royal control over the region. The family of the High Priests of Amun at Thebes maintained a purely nominal claim to the title of Viceroy, but in practice Nubia and its people were left to their own devices.

The three centuries which followed the collapse of Egyptian authority constitute one of the most obscure phases of Nubian history. Written sources are non-existent and the attribution of archaeological material to this period is a matter for debate. The region may have broken up into several chiefdoms. The most important site for the history of this period is el-Kurru, a short distance downstream of Gebel Barkal, where Reisner excavated a Nubian royal cemetery in 1918–19. Egyptian objects of late New Kingdom type found in some of the el-Kurru graves may suggest that this became the power-base of a local ruler soon after the Egyptian withdrawal in the eleventh century BC. The early history of this state has yet to be pieced together, and it is only in the eighth century BC that a clearer picture begins to emerge.

5 Egypt under Kushite Rule

In the eighth century BC a new and powerful Kushite kingdom emerged in the region of Napata, downstream of the Fourth Cataract. The native princes who ruled this state laid the foundations of what was to become the greatest and most sophisticated civilisation of ancient Nubia, the Kingdom of Meroe. Altogether it was to endure for over a thousand years, but some of the major events which determined the course of its development took place during the first half of its existence, the Napatan Period.

The immediate ancestors of these rulers were buried at el-Kurru, in tombs consisting of a tumulus or *mastaba* (a flat-topped rectangular superstructure characteristic of early Egyptian tombs) erected over a burial pit. Although the chronology of these graves is conjectural, the earliest may date back to the end of the New Kingdom, when the Egyptian imperial government was withdrawn from Nubia, as mentioned in the previous chapter. None of the early rulers are known by name, as no contemporary inscriptions have been found, but on later monuments a 'chieftain' named Alara is credited with the foundation of the line of distinguished monarchs, of whom Taharqo is the most famous.

Egyptian influence on the lives and customs of these people seems at first to have been limited. The use of circular tumuli and the laying of the corpse on a bed reflect the strongly African cultural background of the earlier rulers. The effects of the pharaohs' acculturation policy in the New Kingdom appear to have been lost during the following centuries.

The state seems to have developed into a formidable power quite rapidly. By the second half of the eighth century BC the rulers had consolidated their hold on Nubia by means of which nothing is known, and were openly adopting a policy of territorial expansion. In a short time they had acquired a strong measure of Egyptianisation, one of the chief manifestations of which was a devotion to the god Amun. Egypt itself at this time was riven by political disunity, a situation which the Kushites were able to exploit.

Kashta, the first ruler of this line to have left any contemporary inscriptions, secured control of the territory as far north as Elephantine, and he or his successor Piye (a name formerly read 'Piankhy') came to an agreement with the rulers of the Theban area, who perhaps swore allegiance to Kush in return for military support. A few years later, in about 728 BC, the territorial ambitions of Tefnakht, ruler of Sais in the Delta, threatened the independence of Upper Egypt and provided the pretext for Piye to send an army northwards. One by one the cities north of Thebes surrendered or were reduced by siege, and the local rulers who had resisted the Kushite advance submitted to Piye. The various incidents of the expedition are described with exceptional candour and vividness on a granite stela erected in the temple of Amun at Gebel Barkal. The text, inscribed in Egyptian hieroglyphs, stresses the Nubian king's piety and devotion to Amun, but there are novel touches too, such as Piye's well-known lament that the prince of the besieged city of Khmun (later called Hermopolis by the Greeks) had allowed his horses to starve.

After this successful show of force Piye returned to Nubia, apparently allowing the local dynasts in Egypt to remain in charge of their provinces. But only a brief respite was granted. About thirteen years later Piye's successor Shabaqo invaded Egypt again and brought the whole country firmly under Kushite control. Shabaqo (c.716–702 BC) and his three successors Shabitqo, Taharqo and Tanutamani, regarded themselves as legitimate pharaohs of Egypt and were later reckoned as constituting the Twenty-fifth Dynasty. They ruled both Egypt and Kush

44 (*Opposite*) Egypt and Nubia, from the Napatan to the Christian period, showing the principal sites.

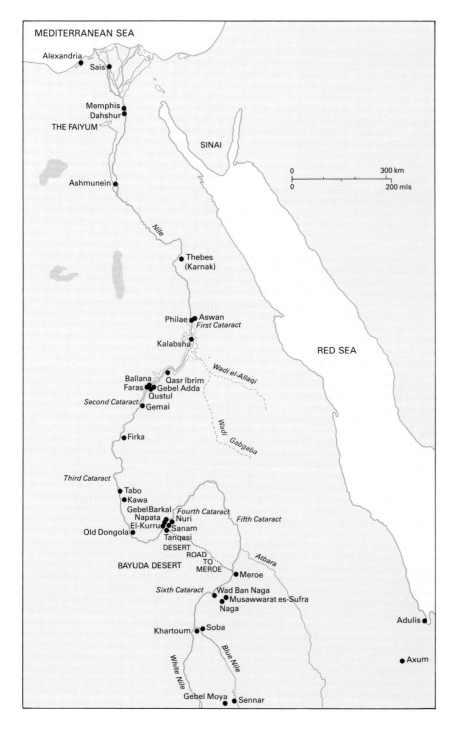

jointly for about fifty years, bringing much-needed peace and stability to the northern kingdom. They posed as true Egyptian pharaohs, ruling with the support of Amun, and they adopted Egyptian royal costume, pharaonic titularies and Egyptian royal burial customs. Nonetheless, they retained their Nubian names, had their southern physical traits represented in sculpture, and adhered to a Nubian tradition of royal succession, by which the throne sometimes passed from the king to his brother.

Despite their southern origins these kings displayed great respect and enthusiasm for the traditions of Egypt. Their intention was to restore Egypt to the greatness it had enjoyed during the prosperous days of the Old, Middle and New Kingdoms. They imposed a strong government, pursued an active foreign policy and stimulated a revival of art, architecture and religious practices, turning repeatedly to 45 the great ages of the past for inspiration.

The government of the country was based at the two centres of Memphis and Thebes. Memphis, which had been a major focus of resistance to Piye's invasion, was made the king's principal residence. The southern region, centred on Thebes, was placed under the control of a princess of the royal house, with the title 'God's Wife of Amun', a religious 46 office of long standing, the holder of which was symbolically the spouse of the supreme state deity. The God's Wives were celibate and each in turn adopted as her successor another young female member of the royal family, thus ensuring that the dynasty retained political power. The God's Wives were assisted by a chief steward and a hierarchy of lesser officials, some of whom were probably Nubians. As an additional means of gaining a firm grip on Egypt in the early stages of their rule the Kushite kings appointed fellow-countrymen to a number of important posts in the civil and religious administration. Complete unification

45 (*Above*) The 'Shabaka Stone'. One manifestation of the interest in Egypt's past which the Kushites stimulated was the study and preservation of religious documents of earlier periods. The text carved on this slab purports to be a copy of an ancient theological composition concerning the creation of the universe, which King Shabaqo ordered to be preserved for posterity. The surface damage to the stone resulted from its having been used as a mill-stone. L. 1.37 m.

46 (*Left*) Statuette of Amenirdis I, daughter of the Kushite ruler Kashta, who was installed at Thebes in the office of God's Wife of Amun in the late eighth century BC. The maintenance of this important post in the hands of the royal family was a major feature of the Kushite domination of Egypt. H. 28.3 cm.

of Egypt was not, however, achieved. In the Delta the numerous local dynasts remained in charge of their principalities throughout the Twenty-fifth Dynasty, a situation which the Kushite rulers perhaps tolerated as it posed no serious threat to their authority.

Compared to what is known of Egypt, information about the organisation of Nubia in this period is extremely meagre. Lower Nubia probably remained virtually uninhabited and apart from minor temple-building by Taharqo the rulers seem to have shown no interest in the area. The two most important towns in the land, Napata and Meroe, lay in Upper Nubia. While Napata, close to Gebel Barkal, was undoubtedly the main religious centre, it is not clear which was the chief administrative base and it may well be that, as in Egypt, both were royal residences of equal importance. Meroe, situated in the area now known as the Butana, between the Atbara and the Blue Nile, was eventually to become the chief city of the land and though evidence is scanty it may have been important from the very foundation of the kingdom; some scholars believe that the royal family originated there before moving north to Napata in the eighth century BC. It is assumed that the economy of Upper Nubia was based on agriculture and animal husbandry as in the past, but the culture of the ordinary people remains almost unknown.

The reign of Taharqo (690–664 BC) marked the high point of the Twenty-fifth Dynasty. The early part of his reign was relatively peaceful, though not without the occasional crisis. A prolonged drought in his sixth year caused a famine which threatened to result in terrible suffering. So serious was the outlook that the king intervened personally, addressing prayers for help to several Egyptian gods. The drought was ended by an exceptional downpour of rain in Nubia, which swelled the Nile and produced an unusually rich harvest.

47 Surviving column of the entrance colonnade in the first court of the temple of Amen-Re at Karnak. The colonnade was one of four erected by Taharqo. 47

The inscription in which this miraculous deliverance was recorded is unique in the literature of Egypt and Nubia in ascribing the flooding of the Nile to natural causes.

Another inscription, found near Dahshur and probably set up early in Taharqo's reign, emphasises the importance of the army in the Kushite state and also illuminates an appealing facet of Taharqo's personality. It describes a demanding military exercise in which the king's troops performed a 'cross-country' run of about thirty miles (forty-eight km) across the desert from Memphis to the Faiyum. To avoid the heat of the sun it took place at night. Taharqo accompanied the army the whole way on horseback. A spirit of competition was instilled into the men and the king rewarded both the winners and the runners-up, 'for His Majesty liked the struggle performed for him.'

Taharqo was the greatest builder of his line and many new religious structures were erected in Egypt in his reign. Thebes received the greatest attention. At Karnak he erected four colonnades at the entrances to the principal New Kingdom temples, of which that in the first court of the temple of Amun, with its majestic standing column, is the best preserved. In Nubia the king constructed a series of temples all of similar design at Gebel Barkal, Kawa, Tabo and Sanam. The Nubian temples, like all those erected by the Twenty-fifth Dynasty monarchs, were thoroughly Egyptian in structure and style of decoration.

The Kushite rule saw a great revival of artistic production in Egypt, and much royal and private sculpture in hard stones survives from this period. The art shows a mixture of influences, that of pharaonic Egypt being the strongest. In sculpture in the round and in temple reliefs, kings and God's Wives are represented in the same idealised forms and engaged in the same religious ceremonies as their immediate Egyptian predecessors. At the same time the Kushites seized upon an already prevalent trend towards drawing inspiration from the art of Egypt's more remote past, introducing a clear archaising element in the products of their time. Moreover, they brought to sculpture and relief a 'southern' element all their own, which shows in the vigour and unprecedented realism of some of their works, 50 together with an emphasis on the ethnic features of the Nubians.

Interest in the past led to monuments of earlier periods being carefully studied. Particularly admired works were copied faithfully. Some of the reliefs in the temple of Taharqo at Kawa, which was built by architects specially sent from Memphis, were copied in every detail from still-existing scenes in Old Kingdom royal mortuary temples in the Memphite necropolis. But other sculptors employed an eclectic approach which went far beyond mechanical copying. Features drawn from models of Old, Middle and New Kingdom date were mixed together and juxtaposed with innovations, one of the most crucial of which was the use of a new canon of proportions for representing the human body. This mingling of different elements shows up in both royal and private sculpture. A number of statues of Taharqo and Tanutamani from Gebel Barkal have the powerfully modelled bodies and simple costumes familiar from Old Kingdom models, yet the torsos have a marked middle line characteristic of Middle Kingdom sculpture. An even more striking example of the fusion of different influences is the sphinx of Taharqo from Kawa, in the British Museum. In its basic form this sculpture is a traditional manifestation of Egyptian kingship but in the depiction of the lion's mane around the king's face the sculptor has drawn on very old models, the finest examples of which date to the Twelfth Dynasty. The bold carving of the face, in which the distinctive Nubian features are strongly marked, lends the piece a vigour and realism which is one of the hallmarks of the finest

48 (*Above left*) Bronze figure of a kneeling Kushite king, perhaps Taharqo, wearing the skull-cap and headband characteristic of Nubian rulers. From Temple 'T' at Kawa. H. 11.2 cm.

49 (*Above right*) Bronze figure of an unidentified Kushite king presented an image of the goddess Maat. The statuette probably formed part of a group representing the king standing before a deity. He wears a necklace with three pendants in the form of ram's heads. From Kawa. H. 16.3 cm.

48, 49

52 (*Opposite bottom*) Foundation deposit from the pyramid of King Senkamanisken at Nuri, comprising tablets of copper, bronze, gold, jasper, lapis lazuli, chalcedony, faience and aragonite, each inscribed with the king's cartouche.

Napatan art. One feature present here which is peculiarly characteristic of sculpture of this period is the pronounced furrow at each side of the nose – the so-called 'Kushite fold'.

Fine work in bronze was done during this period and numerous statuettes of the Kushite kings in this material have survived. They are usually depicted standing or kneeling in the act of making an offering, and most of them probably formed parts of small-scale groups which also included the image of a deity. Three bronze figures of kings from a temple at Kawa are in the British Museum. The kneeling one, uninscribed but attributed to Taharqo on stylistic grounds, illustrates a number of typical features of representations of Kushite kings, such as the double uraeus, or serpent, at the forehead (only one was customary in depictions of Egyptian kings). The headdress worn by this figure appears in many depictions of Kushite rulers. It consisted of a close-fitting

skull-cap, around which was a band of cloth tied at the back and long streamers. This seems to have been the headgear which these kings particularly favoured, although they are also shown wearing the traditional Egyptian crowns and wigs. Another item of royal regalia which seems to have been purely Kushite is a cord-like necklace bearing pendants in the form of rams' heads, depictions of Amun in the form worshipped at Napata.

As might be expected, Egyptian traditions heavily influenced the burial practices of the Napatan rulers. Though they were buried in Nubia at el-Kurru and Nuri, close to Napata itself, all the kings from Piye onwards adopted the pyramid form for the superstructures of their tombs, a custom which was to persist in Nubia for the next thousand years. The models were probably the small brick pyramids erected over New Kingdom private tombs, rather than the great stone edifices of the Old Kingdom. At any rate the Napatan pyramids were modest in size and had steeply sloping walls. Some had a chapel on the eastern side. The tombs were founded according to the ritual practices used in Egypt, which involved the burying of 'foundation deposits' to provide magical protection for the building, and the burials were placed in a subterranean chamber entered via a long descending stairway. Piye, Shabaqo and Shabitqo were buried on beds placed on stone or masonry platforms with niches to accommodate the bed-legs but, beginning in the reign of Taharqo, the kings adopted the Egyptian custom of using coffins and sarcophagi; two famous stone sarcophagi of later Napatan rulers, Anlamani and Aspelta, were faithful copies of Egyptian models. The bodies were mummified and the Egyptian custom of providing *shabti* figures was adopted. Some Nubian customs were retained, however. The strong interest which the Kushite rulers showed in horses is reflected in the practice of

50 (*Above*) Sandstone ornament representing the head of a ram supporting the solar disc, the form in which Amen-Re was usually worshipped at Gebel Barkal. From Kawa. H. 7.4 cm.

51 (*Above*) The pyramid of Taharqo at Nuri. Taharqo was the first Kushite king to be buried here, and his example was followed by nineteen of his successors and fifty-three queens. The pyramids, now partly ruined, were built of sandstone blocks and a funerary chapel adjoined the eastern side. In the richest graves the walls of the subterranean burial chambers were decorated with funerary scenes and inscriptions based on Egyptian models.

burying the king's chariot-horses in a special cemetery close to the pyramids at el-Kurru. The graves consisted of pits in which the horses were buried standing up in groups of four.

The Kushite rulers' ambitions to restore Egypt's greatness led them to interfere in affairs in Palestine. They supported Hezekiah, King of Judah, against the Assyrians and in 701 BC a Kushite army commanded by the young Taharqo fought against the troops of Sennacherib at the Battle of Eltekeh. These acts of intervention proved to be unwise in the long term and culminated in the loss of Egypt by the Kushites. Throughout the second half of Taharqo's twenty-six-year reign the Egypto-Kushite forces were repeatedly engaged in attempts to resist the Assyrian conquest of Egypt. A first invasion, launched by Esar-haddon in 674 BC, was repulsed but a second attempt in 671 succeeded. Memphis fell to the invaders and Taharqo was forced to flee, though his queen and his son were captured. Taharqo returned after the Assyrians with-drew, but the struggle was renewed by Esar-

54

53 Shabtis of Taharqo from his pyramid at Nuri. Taharqo's shabtis were exceptionally large and were made of black granite, serpentine and calcite. The rugged carving of the body and facial features, and the use of an obsolete version of the shabti-formula for the inscriptions, reflect the influence of models dating back to the Middle and New Kingdoms. H. of tallest figure 52.5 cm.

haddon's successor Ashurbanipal in 667/6. Taharqo was again expelled and the Egyptian local dynasts submitted to Assyrian rule. A plot to reinstate Taharqo failed and in 664 he died in Nubia and was laid to rest, with the splendour befitting the ruler of two powerful lands, in his pyramid tomb at Nuri.

This was in effect the end of Kushite rule in Egypt and although Taharqo's successor Tanutamani promptly invaded the northern kingdom he enjoyed only a brief triumph. The invasion, and the execution of Necho, the wily dynast of Sais in the Delta, who had sworn allegiance to Assyria, brought swift retribution. Ashurbanipal sent an army to Egypt and drove Tanutamani back into Nubia, where he spent the remainder of his reign. The Assyrian host sacked Thebes before turning their backs on Egypt for the last time.

Tanutamani's successors continued to rule their ancestral homeland, but through their use of the title 'King of Upper and Lower Egypt'

54 Part of an ornamental painted brick from Nimrud showing an episode in the invasion of Egypt by the Assyrian king Esarhaddon, 671 BC. The slain warrior is identified as a Kushite by the feather in his hair (after Layard, *Monuments of Nineveh* II, pl.53).

55 (*Below*) Steatite shabti of King Senkamaniken (643–623 BC), grandson of Taharqo. His pyramid at Nuri yielded 1277 shabtis (over 3 times the average for an Egyptian burial of this period). After his reign all Nubian royal shabtis were made of faience and a decline in quality is apparent. H. 19.4 cm.

56 (*Below right*) Faience shabti of Queen Nasalsa, wife of Senkamaniken. H. 18 cm.

they maintained the pretence of being the rightful rulers of Egypt as well. The northern kingdom had thrown off the Assyrian yoke within a few years of the sack of Thebes and the country had been reunified and launched into a phase of great prosperity by Psamtek I, son of Necho of Sais. The Saite kings evidently regarded the Kushite pretenders as a threat and hostilities broke out in the reign of Psamtek II. This pharaoh had the names of the Kushite rulers erased from Egyptian monuments and in 593 BC he invaded Nubia. The Kushite troops were defeated in battle in the region of the Third Cataract, and Napata was probably sacked by the victors.

This evidently put an end to Nubian aspirations to regain Egypt, and during the next three hundred years the rulers seem to have concentrated chiefly on affairs within their southern domains. Inscriptions of several kings from Anlamani (*c.*623–593 BC) to Nastasen (*c.*335–315 BC), found at Gebel Barkal and Kawa, describe conflicts in Upper and Lower Nubia and campaigns against desert nomads. A particularly troublesome group, who were to figure repeatedly in the later history of Lower Nubia, were the Blemmyes. These nomads from the Eastern Desert may have been the descendants of the Medjay, and are certainly to be identified with the modern Beja tribesmen.

The rulers seem to have made Meroe their chief residence as early as the sixth century BC, though Napata remained the main religious centre. Several kings down to the reign of Nastasen travelled there to have their kingship confirmed in the temple. Otherwise, apart from occasional visits to attend religious ceremonies, they went to the area only after death, to be buried under their pyramids in the 55, 56 cemetery of Nuri.

6 The Meroitic Period

The Kushite kingdom reached its culmination in the period from c.300 BC to the fourth century AD. Although no distinct historical break with the Napatan Period is recognisable, important changes in the state and culture of the kingdom can be discerned.

As already mentioned, the city of Meroe seems to have been an important Kushite royal residence as early as the eighth century BC. From the beginning of the third century BC Meroe's status as a major centre of the kingdom was greatly strengthened by the abandonment of the custom of burying the rulers at the cemeteries close to Napata; henceforth most royal burials took place at Meroe itself. Coinciding with this new departure there was a gradual shift away from the strong influence of pharaonic Egypt, and a distinctive new culture emerged in which deeply rooted southern elements, mixed with Graeco-Roman influences, played an increasingly strong role. This change is apparent not only in the character of the monarchy, in religion and burial customs and in the arts, but also in the introduction of a written form of the native language.

Meroe lay on the east bank of the Nile midway between the Fifth and Sixth Cataracts. The site, which lies close to the village of Begarawiya, extends over a vast area, the city ruins alone occupying about a square mile. Only a small part has been excavated; among the structures revealed are a great temple dedicated to Amun, approached along an avenue of stone rams, and a large enclosed area dubbed the 'Royal City' by John Garstang, who conducted the first systematic excavations at the site in 1910–14. Within the stone walls of this compound stood structures identified as palaces, a water-sanctuary, administrative buildings and several temples. The houses of the ordinary people are probably still concealed beneath the extensive mounds which cover much of the ancient site. Other temples were located at a distance from the town centre and to the east of the city lay large cemeteries, containing the tombs of the rulers and their subjects.

Meroe was a flourishing centre of industry, and the smelting furnaces and great mounds of slag found at the site testify to the existence of a major iron-making factory. Those who first examined these remains, overestimating the importance of the industry, saw Meroe as the main centre from which knowledge of iron-smelting was diffused through sub-Saharan Africa. Though iron production at Meroe is now considered to have been of only limited influence, the site is of great interest as one of the few identifiable centres of the industry in this part of Africa.

The shift of the kingdom's main power base to Meroe was not accidental. The city occupied an extremely favourable economic position, lying in a fertile area of grassland which benefited from annual rainfall and which was much better situated for agriculture and animal husbandry than the region of Napata. The growing of crops, chiefly barley and millet, and the breeding of cattle seems to have formed the mainstay of the economy. To ensure sufficient water for drinking and for cultivation large reservoirs known as *hafirs* were dug to catch the water which fell during the rainy season. These installations, which are found at several major sites in the Butana, consist of a basin excavated in the earth, sometimes surrounded by statues of lions or frogs, perhaps set up magically to promote fertility. The logistics of constructing such reservoirs presuppose the existence of a highly organised labour-force: one *hafir* at Musawwarat es-Sufra measures about 250 m in diameter and its construction involved the removal of an estimated 250,000 cubic metres of earth.

But the prosperity of Meroe must have been due largely to its position close to several very old-established and important trade routes, some passing northwards from central Africa, others running eastwards to the Red Sea and the Eastern Desert and westwards towards Kordofan and Darfur. The fertile plains of the 'Island of Meroe' (the somewhat inaccurate name given to the region bounded by the Nile and the Atbara rivers) provided a convenient passage between the barren and inhospitable stretch of the Nile north of the Fifth Cataract and the difficult granite rapids of the Sixth Cataract. Several routes converged at Wad Ban Naga, south of Meroe, where they crossed the Nile before passing through the Bayuda Desert to Napata. A major Meroitic settlement existed at the river crossing, and other important centres, notable today for their striking temples, arose nearby at Naga and Musawwarat es-Sufra.

The political history of Meroe is still imperfectly known. Because of its remoteness from the Mediterranean world foreign visitors were rare, and the kingdom is mentioned only sporadically in the writings of ancient historians – and even then their accounts contain a large measure of fantasy. Herodotus, writing in the late fifth century BC, repeated a fanciful description of the 'Ethiopians' as giants who habitually reached 120 years of age and bound their prisoners in gold chains. Moreover, until the language of Meroe can be understood, much information remains inaccessible.

The organisation of the kingdom appears to have followed essentially the same lines as in the Napatan Period. The head of state was usually a king, who was perhaps considered divine as in Egypt. The chronology of the rulers is based mainly on studies of the development of the royal pyramid-complex, plus a few written sources which provide correlations with the well-known chronology of Egypt and Rome; hence the dates assigned to individual reigns are largely conjectural.

Information on the actual system of government is meagre, although what little can be deduced from inscriptions points to the existence of an upper class composed of officials and priests whose titles seem to have been hereditary within a small number of families. Particularly numerous are references to priests of Amun who, as the earthly representatives of the state god, may have held considerable power. Diodorus recorded a tradition – no doubt highly exaggerated – that the Meroitic king had to obey the priests, who could even compel him to commit suicide when he was judged no longer fit to rule. This arrangement is said to have been ended in the early third century BC by one 'Ergamenes' (possibly to be identified with a king Arqamani, known from contemporary inscriptions) who slaughtered the priests and ruled the kingdom as he saw fit.

The army doubtless constituted another very important element of Meroitic society. A strong militaristic tendency is suggested not only by the numerous depictions of rulers holding weapons and sometimes wearing armour, but also by the widespread practice of burying weapons with the dead – notably iron spearheads and archer's 'looses', small stone rings worn on the thumb to protect the skin and increase the tension produced when

57 Stone thumb rings dating to the Meroitic period (left) and the Ballana Period (right). Such rings were used by archers as an aid in drawing the bow, and are also shown worn as an ornament by Meroitic kings and queens in temple reliefs. D. 4.4 cm and 5 cm.

drawing a bow, a characteristic innovation of the Meroitic Period.

To the outsider, the exceptionally high status of women was one of the most intriguing aspects of Meroitic culture. The female members of the royal family had played an important, though still only partially understood, role as early as the seventh century BC, and by the time the Meroitic kingdom was at its height a matrilinear succession seems to have been in operation, the throne passing from the king to the offspring of his sister. Beginning in the second century BC several queens were rulers of the kingdom in their own right, a situation which probably misled the Roman historian Pliny into stating that the Meroites were always ruled by women called Kandake. The word is derived from a title of uncertain meaning (and is incidentally the origin of the modern name Candace). Some of the queens are depicted on royal monuments as being very fat; since goddesses are always shown with slender figures, even when in the company of the queen, this curious obesity may indicate the leisured earthly existence associated with high status.

Relations with Egypt, which had been insignificant in the period following Psamtek II's campaign, were re-established by the third century BC when the Ptolemaic rulers began to expand trade contacts in the western Mediterranean. This created an increased demand for southern goods such as ivory, spices, exotic animals and slaves, which the Meroites exported to Egypt in return for food supplies and manufactured goods. Apart from a brief period of animosity in the early second century BC, good relations between the two powers seem to have continued for the duration of the Ptolemaic dynasty, one manifestation of which was the collaboration between Ptolemy IV and the Meroitic King Arqamani in the construction of temples at Philae and Dakka. The majority of temple-building and trading activity at this period took place in the Dodekaschoenos, a stretch of the Nile valley immediately south of Aswan which was technically the estate of the temple of Isis at Philae but was in practice under Egyptian royal control. This strategically important region also gave access to the Wadi el-Allaqi gold mines, which were reopened under the Ptolemies. Attempts by the Meroites to seize control of this area brought them into conflict with the expanding power of Rome late in the first century BC. Between 30 and 28 BC the Romans conquered the whole of Egypt as far south as Aswan, and the Dodekaschoenos, though not occupied, was declared a protectorate so as to give the Romans control of the gold resources.

What happened next was described in detail by the Greek historian Strabo. Taking advantage of the withdrawal of Roman forces for a campaign in Arabia in 25–24 BC, the Meroites launched an attack and sacked Philae, Elephantine and Aswan, where they destroyed statues of Augustus. The Romans quickly retaliated: Gaius Petronius, Prefect of Egypt, defeated the Meroitic army in a punitive campaign which culminated in the sack of Napata. A garrison of four hundred Roman troops was stationed at the outpost of Qasr Ibrim. The Meroites submitted and at the Treaty of Samos a permanent frontier between Meroe and Roman Egypt was established at Maharraqa (Hierasykaminos), leaving the Dodekaschoenos under Roman control.

The conclusion of hostilities inaugurated a long period of peace, during which Meroe enjoyed profitable commercial relations with Rome. Both in Upper and Lower Nubia graves of this period contain large quantities of pottery, bronzework, glass and silverware imported not only from Roman Egypt but from other centres as far afield as Pergamon and Algeria, and the influence of Mediterranean fashions left an indelible imprint on the culture of the southern kingdom. The Meroites, for

58 (*Right*) Bronze head from a statue of Augustus thought to have been taken as plunder by the Meroites during their reign on Aswan. It was discovered buried in clean sand in front of a small temple in the 'Royal City' at Meroe, possibly erected to commemorate the raid. H. 48.2 cm.

59 (*Far right*) Part of a Roman catapult quarrel found at Qasr Ibrim. The historically documented presence of a Roman garrison at the outpost of Qasr Ibrim in the last quarter of the first century BC has been confirmed by the discovery of well-preserved objects of Roman type. In its design this object is identical to other examples from the Augustan period and may be associated with the occupation of the site by Petronius' garrison. L. 13.3 cm.

60 (*Right*) The fortified stronghold of Qasr Ibrim as it appeared in the early nineteenth century, shortly after its final abandonment in 1812. Qasr Ibrim was an outpost of great strategic importance and was occupied probably as early as the New Kingdom. (After Belzoni, *Plates illustrative of the Researches and Operations of G. Belzoni in Egypt and Nubia*, London, 1820, pl.27).

61 (*Far right*) Roman shoes from Qasr Ibrim. In addition to footwear, coins, lamps and other pieces of military equipment have been unearthed at the site. The large quantity of such material may indicate that the occupation of the outpost continued into the first century AD. L. of both 25 cm.

their part, continued to export the perennially desirable gold, ivory and ebony. A store of ebony logs and elephant-tusks, found in a chamber of the so-called 'palace' at the important trade depot of Wad Ban Naga, probably represents a consignment destined for Egypt, abandoned for some reason now unknown.

As the kingdom flourished its sphere of influence grew. The southern limits of Meroitic control are unknown, but an outpost existed at Sennar on the Blue Nile and trade was carried on with the people of Gebel Moya, in the Gezira south of Khartoum, the site of a culture of a strongly African character. In the north the large area of Lower Nubia south of the frontier at Maharraqa had remained virtually uninhabited throughout the first millennium BC; from the beginning of the first century AD, however, settlement was re- 62 established there largely as a consequence, it is believed, of the introduction of the ox-driven water wheel or *saqia*, which dramatically increased agricultural productivity.

Meroitic occupation at Lower Nubian sites

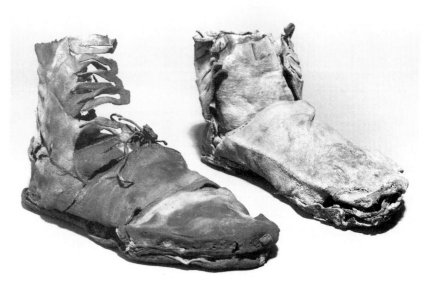

such as Faras perhaps began as early as the first century BC but the region probably did not become densely populated until after the time of Christ. In contrast to the Dodekaschoenos, which was culturally part of Egypt, the rest of the territory below the Second Cataract was entirely Nubian in character. Civil and religious control was in the hands of a few Meroitic families, under the authority of the *Pesato*, an official who functioned as a viceroy with Faras as his main administrative centre. The rest of the population appears to have been a mixture of Meroitic-speaking people from the south and other elements who perhaps moved in from the regions to the east and west. Some of these newcomers – possibly the majority – spoke an ancestral version of the modern Nubian language and were to play a significant role in events following the collapse of Meroitic authority.

From the second century BC the Meroites began to produce inscriptions in their native tongue rather than in Egyptian, which had been the only written language used in the Napatan Period. Meroitic was written in two scripts, one using twenty-three symbols 63 adapted from Egyptian hieroglyphs but with different sound-values, the other a shorthand 64 form referred to as 'cursive', a somewhat inappropriate title since the signs are not joined. At least some of the cursive signs were derived from Demotic, the everyday script of Egypt in the Ptolemaic and Roman periods. Unlike Egyptian, Meroitic was syllabic (vowel-sounds were included) and words were divided first by triple and later by double dots.

The use of Meroitic hieroglyphs was restricted mainly to inscriptions on the walls of temples and tomb chapels, but texts written in the cursive script are much more numerous. These occur as graffiti and are occasionally found on ostraca (pieces of pottery) and papyri, but the most important sources are the funerary stelae and offering tables set up outside

the graves of important individuals. All that can be deduced about these standardised texts is that they begin with an invocation to Isis and Osiris, continue with the owner's name, titles and parentage, and conclude with a prayer for offerings.

The scripts were deciphered by the Egyptologist Francis Llewellyn Griffith about 1909. The 'key' was provided by a bilingual text on a stand for a divine barque, found at Wad Ban Naga. This gave the names of the royal dedicators in both Egyptian and Meroitic hieroglyphs, enabling Griffith to establish sound-values for the latter. He was able to test his theory and to discover the values of the signs not present on the stand by a comparative study of the funerary formulae on the offering tables and stelae. Unfortunately, bilingual inscriptions are rare and none are lengthy enough to provide the basis for a complete understanding of Meroitic grammar or to build up a vocabulary. Although the available texts have been intensively studied by philologists, little significant progress has been made towards understanding their meaning. The problem is exacerbated by the linguistic isolation of Meroitic; it appears to have no surviving relations in Africa and may have belonged to a self-contained group of languages now extinct.

The problem of the inscriptions seriously limits any understanding of Meroitic religion. Nonetheless, both northern and southern influences can be detected in the pantheon. Egyptian deities were pre-eminent – the most important, as before, being Amun. His temples at Gebel Barkal were renovated and enlarged and new ones were built at Meroe and other centres. In the reliefs on the walls the king often stands before the god, who is frequently depicted with his ram's head. His name, vocalised in Meroitic as Amani, forms an element in the names of many of the rulers. The Meroites also showed a strong devotion to

the worship of Isis, whose cult inspired a great popular following throughout the Mediterranean world at this time. Her temple at Philae became a major centre of pilgrimage, not only for Meroites but for other Nubian groups such as the Blemmyes.

Several deities of purely Nubian origin were also worshipped, chief among which was the lion-god Apedemak, the principal Meroitic god after Amun. Apedemak had strong warlike associations and is depicted in statuary and relief at many of the major temples in the south of the kingdom. Other popular deities included Arensnuphis and Sebiumeker, a god of creation, who are represented by pairs of statues of Egyptian style, erected at temple entrances and designed to give protection to the building. More obviously African in inspiration was the endowing of elephants with religious significance. There are clear indications of this at Musawwarat es-Sufra, south of Meroe, which is the site of the 'Great Enclosure', the most remarkable religious precinct in the kingdom. The unique layout of this area included temples and a complex arrangement of courts, rooms and passages, the decoration of which includes reliefs and three-dimensional sculptures of elephants. What role they played can only be conjectured; it has been suggested that the Great Enclosure was a major centre for pilgrims, who journeyed there from every part of the kingdom to attend religious festivals; according to an alternative interpretation, the site may be the remains of a royal palace complex.

Funerary beliefs and practices illustrate a progressive weakening of Egyptian influences, which seem to have been perpetuated chiefly by the royal family and the upper classes. The rulers were buried under pyramids, which were smaller and less well built than those of their Napatan predecessors. The reliefs decorating the walls of the associated chapels strongly reflect Egyptian concepts of the after-

contents page

65 The 'Great Enclosure' at Musawwarat es-Sufra with the statue of an elephant in the foreground. Elephants were used for military purposes, but they also played a religious role in Meroitic culture, the precise significance of which is unclear.

66 South wall of the funerary chapel of pyramid N.11 at Meroe. The owner is believed to have been Queen Shanakdakhete (second century BC), the first female ruler of Meroe, who appears here enthroned with a prince and protected by the wings of the goddess Isis. In addition to the rows of figures carrying palm branches and bringing offerings are ritual scenes including the posthumous judgement of the queen before Osiris. H. 2.52 m.

life. In keeping with this, the bodies were mummified and laid to rest bedecked with gold jewellery and other rich trappings, but the growing influence of African traditions is manifest in the abandoning of the use of *shabti* figures, and a return to the custom of retainer-sacrifice, though on a smaller scale than in the Kerma Culture.

The graves of high-ranking officials and priests had smaller brick superstructures (probably pyramids, though none has survived intact) provided with a small chapel containing an offering table and a funerary stela. Besides the standard formulae addressed to Isis and Osiris many of the offering tables also bear depictions of the Egyptian deities Anubis and Nephthys pouring libations for the benefit of the deceased. In the simpler sepulchres of the ordinary people the body was often laid on a bed in Nubian fashion. Pro-

67 (*Above*) Tomb of a Meroitic private individual at Faras. Only the foundations of the superstructure – probably a brick pyramid – remain. The vaulted brick burial chamber is exposed and to the left are the remains of the funerary chapel with its stone offering table.

68 (*Right*) Offering table from a Meroitic tomb at Faras, inscribed around the edge with a funerary formula in cursive script. The central scene depicts the Egyptian deities Nephthys and Anubis pouring libations for the benefit of the deceased. H. 45.5 cm.

69 (*Far right*) Besides the offering tables free-standing stelae such as this one were set up in Meroitic tomb chapels. Some are round-topped, others resemble offering tables with a redundant 'spout' at the top. The inscriptions, in cursive script, are similar in content to those on the offering tables. H. 36 cm.

70 Relief from the 'Lion-Temple' at Naga showing King Natakamani before the lion-headed god Apedemak and the deities Horus and Amun. The king's long robe with a sash draped over the right shoulder is typical of the Meroitic fashions which increasingly replaced Egyptian royal costume in reliefs.

71 'Ba' statue of a woman. The concept of representing the souls of the dead as human-headed birds derives from Egypt, but the custom of setting up statues of this type outside tombs is known only in Nubia. The majority of examples probably dates to the second and third centuries AD. The sculptures were placed in or above the entrance to tomb chapels on the east side of the superstructure. The simplified treatment of the bodily forms and the prominence given to the eyes is typical of later Meroitic sculpture. H. 46 cm.

visions for the dead were usually lavish and regularly included bronze vessels and jewellery, cosmetic implements, weapons and fine pottery.

The varied influences on Meroitic culture are nowhere more apparent, however, than in its artistic products, which display an eclectic mixture of pharaonic Egyptian, Graeco-Roman and African elements. Relief sculpture, mainly found on the walls of temples and tomb chapels, remained heavily influenced by Egyptian models. Some unusual depictions of Apedemak at the temple of Naga have been thought to reflect Indian inspiration but it is probable that the iconographic models can be traced back to Egypt. Sculpture in the round includes life-size or colossal statues of gods and rulers in typical pharaonic poses and costumes, as well as pieces in a more informal style, such as the figures placed around the pool in the water-sanctuary at Meroe, which combine the relaxed poses of Alexandrian sculpture with a fullness of bodily form

72 'Kiosk' at Naga, showing both Graeco-Roman and Egyptian influence in its architectural details.

characteristic of Meroitic taste. A celebrated example of the mingling of local and Graeco-Roman elements in an architectural context is 72 the 'kiosk' at Naga, with its unique juxtaposition of styles.

A striking and distinct category of Meroitic sculptures are the part-human, part-bird statues set up outside the tombs of persons of high rank in Lower Nubia. The inspiration for these strange figures is the Egyptian concept of 71 the *Ba*, one of the forms which – it was believed – the spirits of the dead could assume. Stylistically the figures reflect a tendency in Meroitic art to reduce the bodily form to its essentials, a

'formalism' which has parallels in modern ethnic sculptures from East Africa.

Among the minor arts, the jewellery is notable for its technical excellence. The techniques mastered by the craftsmen included cloisonné work, granulation and embossing – all of which are exemplified in the most famous collection of Meroitic jewellery, the hoard of gold bracelets, finger-rings, earrings and collars discovered by G. Ferlini in the pyramid of Queen Amanishakheto in 1834 and now in the Munich and Berlin museums. The pharaonic traditions apparent in some Meroitic jewellery are obvious in pieces such

73 Gold ornament representing a canine, possibly a jackal. Though reputedly found near Cyrene in Libya, it is undoubtedly of Meroitic work and is closely paralleled by other examples found in the pyramid of Queen Amanishakheto (first century BC). H. 3.1 cm.

74 Gourd-shaped vessel of burnished black ware from Meroe, first century BC–first century AD. H. 18.5 cm.

as the gold jackal in the British Museum, which is closely paralleled by examples from the queen's treasure.

Fine work in bronze was also produced. In addition to the huge heavy anklets found in many graves, metalworkers produced a wide range of bronze vessels and lamps copying contemporary Roman forms, and small sculptures showing Egyptian and Classical, as well as Meroitic, influences. The production of high-quality textiles, many of cotton, is well-attested not only by depictions of garments in reliefs but also by actual examples, of which the site of Qasr Ibrim has yielded large quantities.

Unquestionably the finest achievement of the Meroitic craftsmen is the pottery, which is justly celebrated for its technical excellence and aesthetic appeal. The most striking are the wheelmade 'fine' wares – bowls, vases and cups of surprisingly thin fabric, painted in several colours or impressed with small ornamental stamps. Contemporary with these are 'utility' wares made of a coarser red fabric, with a variety of forms including tall amphorae, necked vases and globular pots.

The decoration of these vessels was inspired by Mediterranean traditions. Among the common elements are vine-leaf patterns of Graeco-Roman origin, geometric designs, figures of crocodiles, frogs, snakes, giraffes and occasionally humans, and motifs derived from Egyptian symbols such as the *ankh*, *tyet* and lotus. Although the great variety of decoration makes the precise dating of individual pieces difficult, several 'schools' of pottery painting can be recognised through similarities in the general treatment and iconography of the decoration. It is even possible to identify the work of individual painters by the distinctive techniques and subjects which they favoured.

A large amount of pottery was also imported from Roman Egypt and beyond, and excellent imitations of popular types such as *terra*

75 Group of bronze vessels from Meroitic graves at Faras. The open bowl (right) is decorated with *ankh* signs and a frieze of uraeus serpents. H. of vessel at left 11.5 cm.

76 Decorated Meroitic fine ware cups from Faras. The ornamentation consists of painted designs including *ankhs*, frogs and fantastic animals, and small motifs impressed with a stamp. The handled vessel (centre) carries barbotine decoration. H. of cup at lower left 8.8 cm.

sigillata were produced by Meroitic potters. Besides the abundant wheelmade ware, which was made mainly by men, there were also handmade domestic wares, traditionally produced by women. Black in colour, often highly burnished and copying the shapes of gourds or bags, they belong to a purely African ceramic tradition stretching back to the Kerma and C-Group Cultures and beyond.

The Meroitic civilisation had reached its peak by the first century AD. During the following three hundred years it suffered a long gradual decline, outward manifestations of which are an end to the construction of monumental buildings and a diminution in the size and quality of the royal pyramids. Perhaps most significant of all, imported goods virtually disappeared from tomb equipment, a telling sign of an impoverished and declining economy. After about AD 200 Meroe was forced to compete for Roman trade with the rival kingdom of Axum, in northern Ethiopia. Not only were the Axumites encroaching on several of Meroe's sources of trade goods but commerce via the Red Sea port of Adulis, which lay in Axum's territory, held obvious advantages for the Romans. It gave relatively easy access to the markets of India and avoided the arduous and dangerous overland routes which ran through the Meroitic kingdom. As Rome made increasing use of the Red Sea and Arabian trade routes Meroe was bypassed, becoming a commercial backwater. Her nearest trading partner, Egypt, was also suffering a decline in prosperity, in this case due to Roman overexploitation of her resources. To make matters worse, both trading caravans and settled communities in the Nile valley were increasingly threatened by the nomadic raiders of the desert fringes, whose capacity for disrupting everyday life and commerce was vastly increased by the introduction of the camel in the first century BC.

The final collapse of the once mighty king-

77 Redware amphora from a Meroitic grave at Faras, decorated with painted motifs including the figure of an archer. Probably first century BC. H. 43.5 cm.

dom went virtually unnoticed in the Classical world. The monarchical government continued probably until the early fourth century AD, but by then the state was too weak to resist external pressure and fell an easy prey to the aggression of her enemies. The southern heartland of the kingdom was overrun at about this time by the nomadic tribes of the Noba, moving in from the lands west of the Nile. They occupied the towns and cities in the Butana area, Meroe probably among them. About AD 350 Ezana, the first Christian king of Axum, led a campaign into the region, defeating the Noba in battle near the confluence of the Nile and Atbara rivers. Though he styled himself 'King of Kasu' (Kush) on his monuments, the title was an empty one – and Ezana doubtless knew it. Meroe was no more, and the Noba were left in undisturbed occupation of what had once been the centre of one of Africa's first great civilisations.

78 Meroitic redware vase from a grave at Faras. Probably first century BC. H. 24.7 cm.

7 Christian Nubia

The two centuries between the collapse of the Meroitic kingdom and the official adoption of Christianity represent a transitional phase in Nubian history. It is also something of a 'dark age', and one in which historical texts and archaeological evidence are not always easy to reconcile. In the south the glories of Meroitic civilisation were extinguished. The Noba had a simple tribal society and displayed no interest in perpetuating the skills of art, architecture or writing. Apart from distinctive pottery the only remains which can be attributed to these people are a series of tumulus graves along the Nile from Sennar north to the Fourth Cataract. These monuments typify the 'Tanqasi Culture', named after the principal site of this kind, opposite el-Kurru. The poverty of the grave goods is indicative of a society at once illiterate and poor, yet self-sufficient and having little commercial contact with the lands further north.

In Lower Nubia the transition to a new culture was accomplished more smoothly. Textual evidence indicates that the population in the north between the fourth and sixth centuries AD was a mixed one. Apparently the Nubian-speaking peoples who had gradually infiltrated the region during the preceding centuries became the dominant element in the population as the Meroitic state system weakened. The majority of these people, known as the Nobatae, were probably originally nomads from the west and were perhaps related to the Noba, but besides these there were Blemmyes from the Eastern Desert who had established themselves in the Dodekaschoenos after their constant raids had forced the Romans to withdraw their garrisons north to Aswan at the end of the third century AD. The Blemmyes and the Nobatae were sometimes on hostile terms, as indicated by the one known monumental inscription of the period, written in bad Greek on the wall of the temple of Kalabsha, in which Silko, King of the Nobatae,

records his victories over the Blemmyes.

Corresponding with these developments a new material culture is recognisable in the archaeological record of Lower Nubia. This culture, attested from Aswan to the northern end of the Dongola Reach, was first identified by Reisner, who explained its appearance as the direct consequence of a major ethnic change in the population caused by the appearance of a new people, the 'X-Group'. This interpretation has now been discarded and the term 'Ballana Culture', after the most important cemetery site, is usually substituted for X-Group. It is not possible to distinguish specific Blemmye or Nobataean elements in this culture and it should be regarded as a tradition common to the whole of Lower Nubia.

Several of the main settlements of the Meroitic Period continued to be occupied but the Meroitic tradition of monumental architecture was discontinued and the domestic buildings of the Ballana Period were distinctly inferior, the houses being usually irregular in shape and poorly constructed. This break in the architectural tradition is paralleled by the disappearance of other institutions which the Meroites had perpetuated, such as a state religion and the building of royal pyramid tombs. In place of these there was a rise to prominence of more clearly African traditions, traceable back to the Kerma Culture and beyond. These trends are most clearly apparent in such typical Nubian funerary practices as the use of tumulus graves, bed-burials and retainer-sacrifice.

All these features are found in the tombs of the kings of this period, excavated during the 1930s at Ballana and Qustul, two sites on opposite sides of the Nile near Faras. The tombs, consisting of enormous earth tumuli up to 77 m in diameter, yielded the richest treasure of grave goods ever found in Nubia. The principal burial in each tumulus lay on a wooden bed, equipped with jewellery,

79 Hollow clay stand to support a dish or bowl, found in a cemetery east of the city of Meroe. Objects of this type have been attributed to the Noba, the nomadic people who occupied southern Upper Nubia after the collapse of the Meroitic kingdom. Fourth to sixth century AD. H. 27.7 cm.

80 Silver crown with embossed decoration and garnet and cornelian inlays, found on the skull of a king in an intact tumulus at Ballana. The ram's head with feathered crown, the uraeus serpents and Horus falcons imitate Meroitic motifs derived originally from pharaonic Egypt. Fourth century AD. H. (restored) 30.6 cm.

Horses, camels, sheep, donkeys and dogs were also killed and buried, the horses wearing their saddles and harness with silver trappings and accompanied by their grooms who had been killed beside them.

The precise identity of these 'barbarian' monarchs is debatable, though the most reasonable hypothesis identifies them as the kings of the Nobatae. The extent of their authority and the system of government operating in Lower Nubia at this time are unknown. Other sites, such as Qasr Ibrim, Gemai and Firka, were clearly important centres, but their status in relation to the Ballana monarchy is uncertain.

One fact which is clear is that trade with Roman Egypt was increasing, and the overwhelming influence of Mediterranean imports extinguished the last traces of Meroitic and pharaonic Egyptian ceramic traditions in Nubia. Most locally produced Ballana pottery copies forms used in Egypt which in turn imitate late Roman *terra sigillata*. Among the most typical products of the period are the tall red ware goblets, often decorated with simple 81 blobs or streaks of paint, a pattern which may be derived from the Graeco-Roman vine-leaf motif.

In addition to pottery, glassware and bronzes were being imported, and numerous fine bronze lamps and vessels have been found 82 in Ballana graves. Whether these are all imports or include locally made imitations is open to question. Iron weapons are common in graves and this metal was now widely used for tools. Some of the treasure from the Ballana royal tombs was imported from Egypt, but the royal regalia were evidently of local manufacture and testify to the skills of the artisans in silversmithing and inlay work. Whereas large-scale artistic products such as sculpture were not produced at this time, there was great productivity in the minor arts. The important site of Qasr Ibrim was a major centre for

weapons, bronze and silver vessels, and furni-
80 ture. Embossed silver crowns inlaid with glass and semi-precious stones had been placed on the heads of the principal interments. Other sections of the multichambered burial pits contained provision vessels, tools and weapons of bronze and silver, wooden boxes inlaid with ivory, elaborate bronze lamps and items of personal adornment. The ruler's consort was sacrificed and buried with her husband, as were several retainers, some of them clearly soldiers, who seem to have met their deaths by strangling or by having their throats cut.

81 (*Above*) Ballana pottery from Qasr Ibrim. The tall footed goblets are among the most typical vessel-forms from this period. Fifth to sixth centuries AD. H. of tallest vessel 12.2 cm.

82 (*Below*) Bronze lamp with handle in the form of a horse's head, from a Ballana period grave at Qasr Ibrim. The design was a popular one in the Roman world and similar examples have been found at Pompeii and in a queen's pyramid of the late first to early second century AD at Meroe. This specimen has been dated to approximately the same period and was perhaps valued as an heirloom in the Ballana period. L. 19.6 cm.

industries such as woodworking, leather-working, textile production and basket-making, and large quantities of all these products have been found there.

Despite the gradual disappearance of Meroitic culture in this period the Ballana rulers can in some degree be seen as successors to the Meroitic kings, but their rule also saw the sweeping away of the 'pagan' traditions which had survived from pharaonic Egypt through Meroitic culture. The transitional character of the period is well illustrated by the royal treasures from Ballana and Qustul. Some of the crowns are very similar to examples shown in Meroitic reliefs and are decorated with motifs derived from pharaonic Egypt. On other objects, probably recent imports from Egypt, Christian symbols occur, such as a silver casket with figures of Christ and the Apostles, and 'eucharistic' silver spoons. Although these do not necessarily imply that Christianity was yet a strong force in Nubia, it was clearly gaining a foothold. Although no state religion is known in the Ballana Period, the temple of Isis at Philae continued to be a centre for Nubian pilgrims as late as the fifth century AD, but so greatly did this devotion decline in the next century that the final closure of the temple *c.*AD 540 aroused no serious protest.

By the sixth century AD three distinct kingdoms had emerged. The territory of the Nobatae acquired the status of a political entity, the Kingdom of Nobatia, stretching from the First to the Third Cataracts and with Faras as its capital. To the south lay the Kingdom of Makuria, centred on the site of Old Dongola and exercising control over the Nile valley as far south as the region between the Fourth and Fifth Cataracts. The third kingdom, Alwa, lay still further to the south in the area which the Noba had occupied after the fall of Meroe. Its capital of Soba was situated on the Blue Nile, south-east of Khartoum. It was against this

83 Part of a woollen rug from Qasr Ibrim. The surviving decoration consists chiefly of a row of triangular arches supported on columns. Beneath each arch is a tree. Comparison with related pieces suggests that the rug was made in the Near East, possibly in Egypt. L. 1.91 m.

political backdrop that the official conversion of the Nubians to Christianity took place.

Merchants and monks from Egypt had probably begun to spread the knowledge of Christianity through Nubia by the fifth century AD. While the Ballana monarchs, with their 'barbaric' custom of human sacrifice, can scarcely have been Christians themselves, the presence of objects bearing Christian decorative motifs among their grave goods suggests that they were aware, if not actually tolerant, of the new teaching, and its progressive acceptance by their subjects doubtless smoothed the way for the official mission to convert Nubia which set out from Byzantium in the middle of the sixth century.

This enterprise, instigated by the Emperor Justinian, was politically rather than religiously motivated. The Byzantines sought to enhance the security of their imperial possessions and offer a gesture of support towards Christian allies such as the Kingdom of Axum, whose armies Byzantium had promised to supply with auxiliaries from among the Nobatae and Blemmyes. For the Nubian rulers

there was the incentive that acceptance of Christianity would give them the support of Byzantium or Egypt in their struggles with their neighbours. Missionary activity was complicated, however, by the fact that two rival Christian doctrines were struggling for supremacy in the East at this time.

The main point of contention was whether Jesus possessed both human and divine natures (the 'Dyophysite' view) or one nature which was wholly divine (the 'Monophysite' doctrine). The Dyophysite interpretation was favoured by the Byzantine imperial government, while the Monophysite was considered heretical. The latter, however, had a powerful supporter in the person of the Empress Theodora, wife of Justinian. Missionaries from both doctrines were sent to Nubia but it was the Monophysite party which proved the more successful. According to a contemporary but biased account written by John, Bishop of Ephesus, the Dyophysite mission was delayed in Egypt by a trick, enabling the rival party to reach the goal first. Nobatia was the first of the three kingdoms to be converted, by the priest

Julian in about AD 543, and the task was completed by another missionary, Longinus, who was afterwards invited by the King of Alwa to bring the new teaching to his domain as well. Longinus reached Alwa and baptised the ruler and his subjects about AD 580, though only after making a tough roundabout journey to avoid the kingdom of Makuria. This state, which was openly hostile to its neighbours, adopted the more orthodox Dyophysite form of Christianity, probably as a political move to emphasise its independence. At the beginning of the eighth century Makuria seems to have absorbed Nobatia, thereby creating a single large kingdom stretching from the First Cataract to the Abu Hamed area, or perhaps even further south.

The eight to nine centuries of the Christian era was a period of growth and prosperity in both the political and cultural spheres. One of the immediate benefits of the conversion of the kingdoms was the unifying and strengthening effect it had on Nubia as a whole. The integrity of this consolidation was put to the test within a few decades of the missionary journeys.

The Arabs, following hard on their conquest of Egypt in AD 641, twice attempted an invasion of Nubia, but so fierce was the resistance – in which the famous Nubian archers played a crucial role – that attempts at a takeover were abandoned. There followed in 652 a treaty, known in Arabic sources as the *Baqt*, which, unusually, was a compromise guaranteeing the Nubians independence and freedom in return for an annual tribute of 360 slaves and the obligation to maintain a mosque which had been erected in Old Dongola. This agreement remained in force for six hundred years and enabled the Nubian states to prosper and develop unhindered.

The introduction of Christianity into Nubia marked a break in many ancient traditions. The most far-reaching change was the separation of the institutions of church and state. For millennia the people of Nubia had been accustomed to being ruled by kings who were considered divine and who combined secular and religious authority in one person. Now the king was no longer a god and his control over religious affairs was minimal. The change in status of the rulers is strikingly emphasised by the end of the tradition of the royal burial as a symbol of authority; no tombs of Christian kings of Nubia are known, and it is likely that they were quite modest affairs.

The separation of church and state encouraged the development of a more efficient government and legal system. Information about the organisation of the country comes mainly from Arab writers, and relates chiefly to the more accessible northern kingdom, whose principal royal residence was at Old Dongola, a large town situated in an agriculturally productive stretch of the Nile valley, south of the Letti Basin. As in medieval states generally, the king held absolute power and technically owned all the land in the kingdom. The ordinary people were theoretically regarded as his slaves, though in practice the king could not impose rigid control on them; when some Nubians from the Aswan area sold their lands to Egyptian Moslems in the ninth century the king of the time found himself powerless to prevent them.

Apart from a number of local vassal rulers, of whom little is known, the most powerful official after the king was the 'Eparch', who resided at Qasr Ibrim and acted in the capacity of the king's viceroy for Lower Nubia, perhaps performing a similar function to the *pesato* who had governed the same area in the Meroitic Period. His role was to supervise commercial dealings with Moslem Egypt and to defend the northern frontier of the kingdom. Northern Nubia was once more a kind of buffer zone, but after the ninth century its inhabitants enjoyed a higher standard of living and greater freedom than those in the south. Moslems from Egypt were permitted to enter the area to trade, and some (probably mostly merchants and craftsmen) settled there. They were forbidden to pass beyond the Second Cataract without permission, however, as a safeguard against the infiltration of Islamic influences into the kingdom's heartland, which seems to have remained under strict royal control.

In contrast to the resistance manifested towards Islam the Nubian monarchy was heavily under the influence of Byzantine traditions. The royal robes and trappings of the kings as depicted in paintings from Faras are clearly inspired by Byzantine models, and several of the officials in the service of the kings and eparchs had Greek titles familiar from Byzantine states, though how closely their duties mirrored those of their prototypes remains unknown.

Unlike the relatively well-documented kingdom of Makuria, that of Alwa to the south is still little known. Written sources are vague and though Alwa was described by the tenth-century writer Ibn Selim el-Aswani as a rich and prosperous state, archaeology is only beginning to corroborate this. Its prosperity was perhaps based on slave-trading; the kingdom bordered the 'pagan' lands of Kordofan and the upper reaches of the Nile, giving it convenient access to marketable human resources. The state seems to have been of sufficient commercial importance to attract many Moslem merchants to the captial, Soba. Their presence is mentioned in the writings of Ibn Selim, but excavations have brought to light more tangible evidence in the form of coins and exquisite glass vessels of Islamic manufacture.

The Christian church in Nubia was essentially Monophysite after the seventh century. Following the absorption of Nobatia the Kingdom of Makuria seems to have been content to abandon its adherence to the Dyophysite doctrine, which had perhaps now outlived its usefulness as a focus for opposition to the northern state. Monophysite Christianity also became supreme in Egypt after the Arab conquest and the Nubian church was affiliated with that of Egypt. The Coptic partriarch of Alexandria was acknowledged as its head, and its bishops, though mostly of Nubian birth, were appointed at Alexandria. The bishops, of whom the most prominent were those of the important centres of Dongola and Faras, controlled all religious activity in Nubia.

Faras is the best-known Nubian episcopal site thanks to the discovery of the well-preserved cathedral and bishop's palace by the Polish Archaeological Mission in 1961–4. The cathedral was one of the most impressive religious buildings in Nubia and is chiefly famous for the 169 coloured paintings discovered on its walls. After the thirteenth century, when Faras declined in importance,

84 Painting from Faras Cathedral showing Marianos, Bishop of Pachoras (Faras), AD 1005–36. It is part of a series of portraits of local bishops, the earliest of which date to the ninth century AD.

the bishops normally resided at Qasr Ibrim which had been the site of one of the earliest and finest of the Nubian cathedrals.

The cathedrals represent only one manifestation of the wealth of ecclesiastical buildings erected in Christian Nubia. Churches and monasteries sprang up everywhere and in the later Christian period there were often several churches in a single community. The majority of Nubian churches were small rectangular buildings built of rough stone or brick, often with a vaulted roof. The standard model was the *basilica* type of church usual in the Byzantine empire. This was no accident, for architects skilled in church-building were sent from Byzantium soon after the conversion to offer their assistance. The churches were orientated on an east-west axis, with a central nave and two flanking aisles separated by colonnades. The altar and sanctuary stood at the east end, in front of an internal apse. On either side were small vestries which, in many churches, were connected by a passage of unknown purpose, running behind the sanctuary. Another pair of rooms was often constructed at the western end, creating a layout which in plan resembled a cross within a rectangle.

The extent to which Christianity took root in Nubia is clear from the graves of this period, which exhibit an unprecedented simplicity in keeping with new attitudes to life after death. The provision of funerary offerings ceased and

the body, wrapped in a shroud, was laid in a simple pit grave covered with stones or a brick canopy. Besides individual graves, family vaults were used, the bodies being stacked up unceremoniously inside. Some of the more elaborate graves had brick superstructures and a number of these were provided with tombstones. The burials of clerics were an exception to the general rule of austerity; they were laid to rest in their ecclesiastical robes with symbols of their office, and were sometimes provided with vessels, probably containing holy water. An important example is the burial of Timotheos, bishop of Qasr Ibrim, who was buried in the north crypt of the cathedral in the late fourteenth century. Although the interment seems to have been a somewhat hasty affair and the bishop's robes were of simple design (perhaps his travelling gear), he was buried with his iron benedictional cross and two long paper scrolls inscribed in Coptic, Greek and Arabic, which were in effect his letters of appointment from the patriarch at Alexandria. The clothes of Bishop Timotheos are in the British Museum, as are his other belongings, with the exception of the scrolls which are now in Cairo.

Large-scale artistic production in Christian Nubia is mainly found in religious contexts. Sculpture was rare, and was confined chiefly to carved column capitals, cornices, lintels and relief friezes of stone or wood, which were installed in churches and cathedrals in the early Christian period. Some of the most typical examples, showing the characteristic use of floral and bird motifs, come from Faras cathedral. The masterpieces of Nubian religious art, however, are the murals which began to be painted inside churches from the early eighth century. They show a unique mixture of Byzantine, Coptic and even Syro-Palestinian influences, all skilfully blended together by the native artists to produce a distinctive Nubian school of painting.

85 (*Above*) Iron benedictional cross found on the body of Bishop Timotheos, whose intact burial was discovered in the cathedral at Qasr Ibrim; late fourteenth century AD. H. 32.5 cm.

86 (*Right*) Plan of a typical Nubian church of the Classic Christian period, tenth century AD.

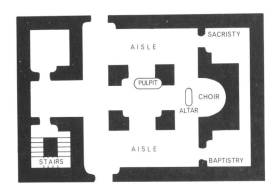

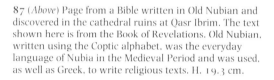

87 (*Above*) Page from a Bible written in Old Nubian and discovered in the cathedral ruins at Qasr Ibrim. The text shown here is from the Book of Revelations. Old Nubian, written using the Coptic alphabet, was the everyday language of Nubia in the Medieval Period and was used, as well as Greek, to write religious texts. H. 19.3 cm.

88 Sandstone tombstone of the lady Nikea from Kalabsha. Tombstones were fixed in the superstructures of graves of well-to-do people in the Christian era. Many examples have been found, often reused in domestic contexts. As here, the inscriptions are usually in Greek, the standard liturgical language of Christian Nubia. H. 18 cm.

89 Section of carved sandstone frieze which formed part of the internal decoration of the first cathedral at Faras, constructed at the beginning of the seventh century AD. The bird has been variously identified as a dove or an eagle, both of which were important symbols in early Christian iconography. H. 25 cm.

Most Nubian churches probably possessed murals but only in a few instances have they been found well preserved. The most famous are those of Faras cathedral, popularly but erroneously known as the Faras 'frescoes' (they are not true frescoes since the paint was applied to a dry plaster surface). Among the most important scenes here are a detailed Nativity, a Crucifixion, and a representation of the archangel Michael protecting the three Hebrews in the furnace. The rest of the paintings are mainly figures of Christ, the Madonna, archangels and saints, together 84 with Nubian kings, eparchs and bishops, usually with inscriptions to identify them. The Faras paintings were successfully removed from the cathedral walls and are now divided between the National Museum of Antiquities in Khartoum, and the National Museum in Warsaw. Several layers of superimposed decoration were carefully separated by conservators, enabling art-historians to re-construct four main phases of stylistic develop-ment, covering a period of five hundred years. The main changes recognisable are in the colours used, which became brighter and less muted, and in the iconography: faces develop from stylised masks to more realistic and individual portraits, while robes and other attributes became more elaborately detailed.

Pottery production is the best documented of the minor arts. The finest type produced in the north was 'Dongola Ware', which had its heyday in the ninth and tenth centuries. The vessels are mainly small bowls with white, 91 cream or buff slip, and are often decorated in the centre with the stamped motif of an animal or a Christian emblem. Others are painted with patterns, bird's heads or crosses. The type shows many similarities with Meroitic painted fine ware but this resemblance is misleading. The illuminated manuscripts of the Coptic Period appear to have been the main inspir-ation for this style of ceramic decoration, as

90 Wooden carving of detailed workmanship showing a scene of baptism. From Qasr Ibrim, twelfth or thirteenth century AD. H. 8.9 cm.

91 Footed bowl of the Classic Christian period (ninth to eleventh centuries AD) from Qasr Ibrim. It has a glossy orange finish typical of the finest Christian pottery from Nubia. H. 13.3 cm.

they also influenced the church murals. The most distinguished ceramic material from the south is the 'Soba Ware' associated with the 92 Kingdom of Alwa. This fine-quality pottery, which has no clear links with ceramics from adjacent regions or from Egypt, is decorated with patterns of dots and rosettes, painted after firing.

Plaited and coiled baskets continued to be made, and large numbers have been found at Qasr Ibrim. The same rich site has yielded abundant evidence of the variety and high quality of the textiles being produced in this period. Besides wool, which was widely used from the Ballana Period, the range of materials was augmented by the appearance of silk and a revival in the popularity of cotton. Several of the garments belonging to Bishop Timotheos

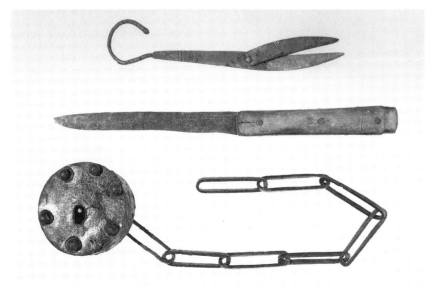

were made of the latter material.

From the eighth to the thirteenth centuries relations between Nubia and Egypt were generally cordial, if fluctuating. The Nubians took advantage of periods of political turmoil in Egypt to launch raids north of Aswan and to renege on their tributary obligations under the terms of the *Baqt*. Retaliation seems to have been comparatively rare but the Nubians received a jolt when, in 1172/73, Shams ed-Dawla, brother of Saladin, invaded Nubia and raided Qasr Ibrim.

After the twelfth century conditions in Nubia became much more unsettled. The influence of the church declined, the authority of the kings was weakened by dynastic infighting, feudal warlords rose to prominence and Arab nomads from the Eastern Desert edge became a serious cause of disruption. The Mamelukes, who took over Egypt in 1260, adopted a more aggressive attitude towards Nubia than their predecessors and interfered in events there more frequently. The troubled state of the land is highlighted by an increase in the building of castles and fortified structures and a corresponding decline in church architecture. Settlements in Lower Nubia were abandoned as the populations withdrew further south or clustered for safety in a few well-defended hill-sites such as Qasr Ibrim and Gebel Adda. The disruption brought in its wake economic decline; commerce and local industry seem to have dwindled almost to a halt, and the pottery of the Terminal Christian Period is among the crudest ever made in Nubia.

92 (*Above left*) Fragments of 'Soba ware' pottery vessels from Soba, capital of the Christian Kingdom of Alwa. W. of largest fragment 10.8 cm.

93 (*Left*) Iron scissors, padlock with chain, and knife with rivetted handle, from Qasr Ibrim. Early to Late Christian, seventh to fourteenth centuries AD. Iron was used to make a wide range of domestic objects from the Ballana Period onwards. L. of scissors, 15 cm.

The northern kingdom finally broke up into hostile principalities in the late fourteenth century, leaving Nubia a prey to nomadic incursions and the aggression of the Islamic rulers of Egypt. In the south the Kingdom of Alwa is traditionally supposed to have been conquered in the early sixteenth century by the ruler of the Funj, a Moslem people who occupied the region south of Khartoum. By this date Christianity was practically extinct in Nubia. The inhabitants, under the influence of the numerous bedouin Arabs who had gained authority throughout much of the country, became part of the Arab tribal system and adopted the religion which had already taken root in many parts of the land, that of Islam.

94 Glass vessel of Islamic manufacture from Soba. A Moslem quarter existed in Soba, capital of the Kingdom of Alwa. It is likely that vessels such as this were imported from Egypt. Probably fourteenth century AD. H. 28 cm.

Further reading

W. Y. Adams, *Nubia, Corridor to Africa*, Princeton, 1977. Repr. with new preface, 1984.

B. G. Trigger, *Nubia under the Pharaohs*, London, 1976.

W. B. Emery, *Egypt in Nubia*, London, 1965.

T. Säve-Söderbergh, *Temples and Tombs of Ancient Nubia*, London, 1987.

G. Connah, *African Civilizations*, Cambridge, 1987.

H. S. Smith and R. M. Hall (eds), *Ancient Centres of Egyptian Civilization*, London, 1983.

B. G. Trigger, B. J. Kemp, D. O'Connor and A. B. Lloyd, *Ancient Egypt, A Social History*, Cambridge, 1983.

The Brooklyn Museum, *Africa in Antiquity: The Arts of Ancient Nubia and the Sudan*, 2 vols, Brooklyn, 1978.

Photographic acknowledgements

The author and publisher are grateful to the following for permission to reproduce their photographs:
Carol Andrews, 43
C. Bonnet, 25
Martin Davies, inside front cover, 70
W. V. Davies, contents page, 34, 51, 72
Egypt Exploration Society, 33
Courtesy of the Griffith Institute, Oxford, 7, 41, 62, 67
Mark Horton, inside back cover
The Illustrated London News Picture Library, 12, 80 (Cairo Museum No. JE 88885)
T. Kendall, 21, 65
A. Marks, 2
National Museum, Warsaw, 84 (No. 234036)
Staatliche Museen, Berlin, 63 (No. 7261)
John H. Taylor, 14, 47
All other photographs have been provided by the Photographic Service of the British Museum and the work of Peter Hayman is particularly acknowledged. Drawn by Christine Barratt, Graphics Officer, Department of Egyptian Antiquities, 1, 16, 26, 44, 86

List of Museum registration numbers

The numbers refer to the illustrations.
Front cover EA 1770
Title page EA 922
Back cover EA 51477
3 EA 921
4 EA 66570, 71809, 71810
5 EA 29433
6 EA 51185
8 EA 51193, 51187, 51188, 51191, 51192
9 EA 51179
10 EA 51199
11 EA 51168, 51169
13 EA 51230
15 EA 852
17 EA 684
18 EA 10752/3
19 (Left to right) EA 51789, 51209, 51226, 51208, 51245
20 (Top to bottom) EA 51242, 51234, 51224, 51241, 51232, 51221
22 EA 55442
23 EA 55444–5
24 EA 55424
27 EA 63027
28 EA 63224
29 (Top to bottom) EA 30849, 63235, 63320, 63319, 63267
30 EA 1835
31 EA 67172–67180
32 EA 1021
35 EA 1279
36 EA 1055
39 EA 64041
40 EA 51259–63
42 EA 1
45 EA 498
46 EA 46699
48 EA 63595
49 EA 63594
50 EA 63611
52 EA 55561
53 EA 55482–9
55 EA 55493
56 EA 55517
57 EA 51560, 65278
58 GR 1911.9–1.1
59 EA 71818
61 EA 71819–20
64 EA 1650
66 EA 719
68 EA 1587
69 EA 901
71 EA 53965
73 EA 68502
74 EA 49388
75 EA 51585, 51593, 51580, 51596, 51462
76 EA 51628, 51627, 51480, 51615, 51635, 51448
77 EA 51515
78 EA 51684
79 EA 49409
81 (Left to right) EA 66560, 67980, 71821, 71822
82 EA 66576
83 EA 66708
85 MLA 1971–8–1, 5
87 EA 71303
88 EA 824
89 EA 606
90 EA 68338
91 EA 71823
92 EA 71813–6
93 (From top to bottom) EA 71824–6
94 EA 71817

Acknowledgements

The author wishes to thank M. L. Bierbrier, W. V. Davies, P. Lacovara, S. Quirke, C. N. Reeves and L. Török for reading the text of this book in manuscript and for providing valuable comments. For any errors or inaccuracies, however, the author alone is responsible.